The Nuremberg Trials

by
Earle Rice Jr.

FAMOUS

TRIALS

Lucent Books, San Diego, CA

Other books in the Famous Trials series:

The Dred Scott Decision
The O.J. Simpson Trial
The Salem Witch Trials
The Scopes Trial
The Trial of Socrates

Library of Congress Cataloging-in-Publication Data

Rice, Earle
  The Nuremberg trials / by Earle Rice Jr.
    p. cm. — (Famous trials)
  Includes bibliographical references and index.
  Summary: Discusses the events leading to the trial of Nazi war criminals after World War II and analyzes both the Allied prosecution and the German defense.
  ISBN 1-56006-269-X (alk. paper)
  1. Nuremberg Trial of Major German War Criminals, Nuremberg, Germany, 1945–1946—Juvenile literature. 2. War crime trials—Germany—Nuremberg—Juvenile literature. [1. Nuremberg Trial of Major German War Criminals, Nuremberg, Germany, 1945–1946. 2. War crime trials .] I. Title. II. Series: Famous trials series.
D804.G42R525 1997
341.6'90268—dc20   96-31426
                                           CIP
                                           AC

Table of Contents

Foreword

"The law is not an end in and of itself, nor does it provide ends. It is preeminently a means to serve what we think is right."

William J. Brennan Jr.

THE CONCEPT OF JUSTICE AND THE RULE OF LAW are hallmarks of Western civilization, manifested perhaps most visibly in widely famous and dramatic court trials. These trials include such important and memorable personages as the ancient Greek philosopher Socrates, who was accused and convicted of corrupting the minds of his society's youth in 399 B.C.; the French maiden and military leader Joan of Arc, accused and convicted of heresy against the church in 1431; to former football star O. J. Simpson, acquitted of double murder in 1995. These and other well-known and controversial trials constitute the most public, and therefore most familiar, demonstrations of a Western legal tradition that dates back through the ages. Although no one is certain when the first law code appeared or when the first formal court trials were held, Babylonian ruler Hammurabi introduced the first known law code in about 1760 B.C. It remains unclear how this code was administered, and no records of specific trials have survived. What is clear, however, is that humans have always sought to govern behavior and define actions in terms of law.

Almost all societies have made laws and prosecuted people for going against those laws, but the question of which behaviors to sanction and which to censure has always been controversial and remains in flux. Some, such as Roman orator and legislator Cicero, argue that laws are simply applications of universal standards. Cicero believed that humanity would agree on what constituted illegal behavior and that human laws were a mere extension of natural laws. "True law is right reason in agreement with nature," he wrote,

4

world-wide in scope, unchanging, everlasting. . . . We may not oppose or alter that law, we cannot abolish it, we cannot be freed from its obligations by any legislature. . . .This [natural] law does not differ for Rome and for Athens, for the present and for the future. . . . It is and will be valid for all nations and all times.

Cicero's rather optimistic view has been contradicted throughout history, however. For every law made to preserve harmony and set universal standards of behavior, another has been born of fear, prejudice, greed, desire for power, and a host of other motives. History is replete with individuals defying and fighting to change such laws—and even to topple governments that dictate such laws. Abolitionists fought against slavery, civil rights leaders fought for equal rights, millions throughout the world have fought for independence—these constitute a minimum of reasons for which people have sought to overturn laws that they believed to be wrong or unjust. In opposition to Cicero, then, many others, such as eighteenth-century English poet and philosopher William Godwin, believe humans must be constantly vigilant against bad laws. As Godwin said in 1793:

Laws we sometimes call the wisdom of our ancestors. But this is a strange imposition. It was as frequently the dictate of their passion, of timidity, jealousy, a monopolizing spirit, and a lust of power that knew no bounds. Are we not obliged perpetually to renew and remodel this misnamed wisdom of our ancestors? To correct it by a detection of their ignorance, and a censure of their intolerance?

Lucent Books' *Famous Trials* series showcases trials that exemplify both society's praiseworthy condemnation of universally unacceptable behavior, and its misguided persecution of individuals based on fear and ignorance, as well as trials that leave open the question of whether justice has been done. Each volume begins by setting the scene and providing a historical context to show how society's mores influence the trial process and the verdict. Each book goes on to present a detailed and lively account of the trial, including liberal use of primary source material such as direct testimony, lawyers' summations, and contemporary and modern commentary. In addition, sidebars throughout the text create a broader context by presenting illuminating details about important points of law, information on key personalities, and important distinctions related to civil, federal, and criminal procedures. Thus, all of the primary and secondary source material included in both the text and the sidebars demonstrates to readers the sources and methods historians use to derive information and conclusions about such events.

Lastly, each *Famous Trials* volume includes one or more of the following comprehensive tools that motivate readers to pursue further reading and research. A timeline allows readers to see the scope of the trial at a glance, annotated bibliographies provide both sources for further research and a thorough list of works consulted, a glossary helps students with unfamiliar words and concepts, and a comprehensive index permits quick scanning of the book as a whole.

The insight of Oliver Wendell Holmes Jr., distinguished Supreme Court justice, exemplifies the theme of the *Famous Trials* series. Taken from *The Common Law*, published in 1881, Holmes remarked: "The life of the law has not been logic, it has been experience." That "experience" consists mainly in how laws are applied in society and challenged in the courts, a process resulting in differing outcomes from one generation to the next. Thus, the *Famous Trials* series encourages readers to examine trials within a broader historical and social context.

Introduction

The Road to Nuremberg

*A*T ABOUT TWENTY MINUTES TO MIDNIGHT *on October 15, 1946, shouts of "Corporal of the Guard!" broke the stillness of the cellblock at Nuremberg, Germany. The sounds of Staff Sergeant Gregory Tymchyshyn's heavy footsteps echoed down the empty corridor, tracing his path to the prison chaplain's office. "Chaplain, chaplain, there's something wrong with Göring!" the sergeant shouted.*

Reverend Henry F. Gerecke and Tymchyshyn returned in haste to cell 5. They found condemned Nazi war criminal Hermann Göring lying on his back, his throat gurgling, his hand dangling over the side of his bed. The Nazi's breathing was labored and loud. His face was green, and froth bubbled from one corner of his mouth. Reverend Gerecke took his pulse and said, "Good Lord, this man is dying." Arriving moments later, Captain Robert Starnes, the chief prison doctor, pronounced the Nazi dead of cyanide poisoning.

Hermann William Göring, imperial marshal of Germany's Third Reich and the second-ranking Nazi next to Adolf Hitler himself, had cheated the hangman's justice at Nuremberg.

Justice or Vengeance?

The Nuremberg hearings, in which twenty-two major Nazi war criminals were brought before the International Military Tribunal (IMT) at Nuremberg, Germany, commenced in November 1945 and extended to October 1946. The IMT was jointly established by the United States, Great Britain, the Soviet

7

Union, and France. This tribunal presided over international war crimes for the first time in the long history of warfare.

More than a half-century later, controversy still rages over the precedents established at Nuremberg, the legality of some of the previously nonexistent charges (created only after the alleged crimes had been committed); and whether the Allies really sought a just judgment or merely to vindictively punish a defeated nation. The verdict of history remains undecided.

News of Nazi War Crimes

News of the Nazis' brutal crimes against humanity began to filter out of occupied Poland as early as January 1940, only slightly more than four months after the start of World War II. At the start of the 1940s, the U.S. Embassy in Berlin reported a mass deportation of German Jews to work camps and farms in Poland.

The Nuremberg Palace of Justice, where the most prominent Nazis were tried. The public's demand to punish the Nazis for their crimes against humanity propelled the trials forward.

Much of the free world refused to believe such revelations. Nevertheless, the Nazis' infamous "Final Solution of the Jewish Problem"—later called the Holocaust—had begun.

On October 25, 1941, U.S. president Franklin D. Roosevelt and British prime minister Winston Churchill released simultaneous statements, publicly deploring German atrocities in the occupied lands. Outraged cries for retribution began to grow in number and intensity in the free world.

The Moscow Declaration

By the end of 1942, most of Europe had fallen under Nazi control. Reports of Nazi atrocities escalated and were borne to the outside world by refugees, neutral travelers, intelligence agents, and others. Although Churchill and Roosevelt agreed that war criminals should stand trial, Churchill thought that the fate of *major* war criminals should be determined by a political decision of the Allied powers. Churchill and many other British officials favored swift execution of major Nazi criminals. They felt that prolonged trials would foment even greater resentment among the German people and delay the postwar healing process. Soviet leader Joseph Stalin disagreed and insisted that *all* war criminals should be tried before "a special international tribunal."

In October 1943 at the Moscow Conference of the Foreign Ministers of Great Britain, the United States, and the Soviet Union, representatives of the three principal Allied nations met to reconcile differences and define a common postwar policy. On November 1, 1943, the Allies issued a unified policy statement on war crimes. In part, the Three Power statement warned:

> At the time of the granting of any armistice to any Government which may be set up in Germany those German officers and men and members of the Nazi Party who have been responsible for or have taken a consenting part in . . . atrocities, massacres, and executions will be sent back to the countries in which their abominable deeds were done, in order that they may be judged and punished according to the laws of these liberated countries and the Governments which will be erected therein.

British prime minister Winston Churchill, U.S. president Franklin Delano Roosevelt, and Soviet premier Joseph Stalin negotiated to agree on which Nazis to prosecute for war crimes.

This policy statement, called the Moscow Declaration, pledged a major Allied commitment to deliver Nazi war criminals "to their accusers in order that justice may be done."

Stimson's Suggestion

In December 1944 during the Battle of the Bulge, Nazi elite troops slaughtered some seventy American prisoners at Malmédy, Belgium. Advancing U.S. and British troops soon uncovered further evidence of Nazi atrocities in western Europe at Belsen, Buchenwald, Dachau, and other concentration camps. Public outcries over Nazi war crimes pressured Allied leaders to finalize a unified postwar policy for dealing with German war criminals.

President Roosevelt favored the concept of holding war criminals accountable for their actions but still disapproved of Churchill's preference for summarily executing the chief Nazi war criminals. In the summer of 1944, U.S. secretary of war Henry L. Stimson persuaded the president that the Nazi leaders should be

THE REASON WHY

During the Battle of the Bulge in the Ardennes Forest, SS troops of Standartenführer (Colonel) Joachin Pieper's Kampfegruppe (battle group) summarily executed some seventy or more U.S. prisoners of war at Baugnez near prewar Malmédy, Belgium. After the war General Josef "Sepp" Dietrich, commander of the German Sixth SS Panzer Army, Pieper, and two others were tried at Dachau in May 1946 for issuing illegal orders. They were convicted and sentenced to death.

At Nuremberg U.S. prison psychologist Captain Gustav M. Gilbert discussed an article in *Stars and Stripes* (U.S. Armed Forces newspaper) on the Dachau trial with Nazi defendants General Alfred Jodl and Nazi SS security chief Ernst Kaltenbrunner. In *Nuremberg Diary*, Gilbert wrote:

> I showed Jodl the article in *Stars and Stripes* on the Dachau trial over the shooting of 500 American PW's in the Bulge at Malmédy and elsewhere. The article quoted Sepp Dietrich as saying that Hitler had ordered the Sixth SS Panzer Army to fight "without any human inhibitions." Jodl said it was entirely out of the question that Sepp Dietrich had received or given any orders to shoot PW's, because then he [Jodl] and [Field Marshal Gerd] von Rundstedt would have known about it and they would not have tolerated it for a moment. As a matter of fact, they had taken some 74,000 (?) Anglo-American prisoners in the Bulge and that proved no such order had been given. He considered Sepp Dietrich an honorable soldier, and one who had, as a matter of fact, ridiculed Himmler's "Nordic superiority" [Aryan pure-blood myth]. Kaltenbrunner came over to defend the SS. Jodl and Kaltenbrunner decided that the thing started with one of Hitler's usual hot speeches in GHQ [general headquarters] to fight without mercy and so on, and this was handed down the line until the local commanders, outdoing each other for the Führer's favor, took it upon themselves not to take any prisoners. Kaltenbrunner gave the speech as he imagined Hitler had given it: Fight with fanatic zeal, stop at nothing, sacrifice for the Fatherland, and show your bloody courage and hardness.

> So that is why the GI's were murdered at Malmédy.

None of the death sentences at Dachau were carried out. Dietrich was paroled in 1955. Pieper, released the following year, was killed in 1976 when his house was fire-bombed.

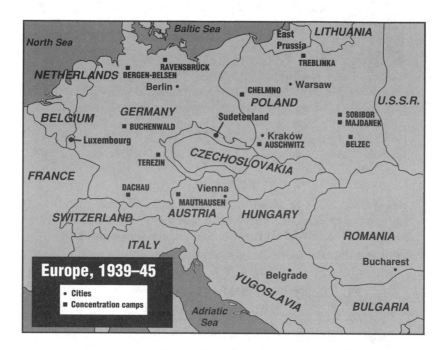

tried before an international tribunal. Stimson argued that to execute Nazi leaders before a firing squad, as Churchill wanted, would imply to a watching world that the Allies were afraid to bring the Nazis to trial. The secretary also pointed out that a war crimes trial would initiate a new age in international affairs in which war was outlawed. Roosevelt concurred, but he would not live long enough to consummate Stimson's suggestion.

On April 12, 1945, with U.S. war crimes plans still far from firm, Roosevelt died at his home in Warm Springs, Georgia.

Hitler's End

History then unfolded dramatically. In an underground bunker fifty feet below the Reichschancellery (German headquarters) in Berlin, German chancellor Adolf Hitler put a pistol to his mouth and shot himself. Eva Braun—his longtime mistress and bride of little more than a day—took poison and joined Hitler in death. It was 3:30 P.M. on Monday, April 30, 1945.

Only a week after Hitler's suicide, Nazi general Alfred G. Jodl signed an unconditional surrender document at General

Dwight D. Eisenhower's headquarters in Rheims, France. The date was May 7, 1945. World War II in Europe ended.

Hitler had eluded Allied punishment for orchestrating and presiding over some of the most heinous crimes ever inflicted upon humanity. Many of his disciples would not.

Executive Order

While representatives of Free World nations were meeting in San Francisco from April 25 to June 26, 1945, to establish the United Nations, Roosevelt's successor, President Harry S. Truman, issued a historic executive order on May 2, 1945. Truman's order designated Robert H. Jackson, associate justice of the Supreme Court, as U.S. chief prosecutor,

> in preparing and prosecuting charges of atrocities and war crimes against such of the leaders of the European Axis powers . . . as the United States may agree with any of the United Nations to bring to trial before an international military tribunal.

With Jackson's appointment, the United States, in hopeful pursuit of justice, took its first step down the long, twisting road to Nuremberg.

Chapter 1

Cries for Justice

DESPITE DIFFERENCES SPANNING CENTURIES of conflict, warring nations have conducted their aggressions within collectively developed and generally adopted rules or limits. These so-called rules of war reflect humankind's well-intentioned but woefully inadequate attempts to minimize the horrors and cruelty of war. In another sense, by adhering to a universally acceptable code of warfare, nations can impose their right to fight with less fear of redress or reprisal. But the laws of war are not binding.

As World War II drew to a close, the world community still lacked any means of enforcing international laws of war or for punishing any nation in violation of them. The problem of how to deal with high-ranking Nazis after peace was restored took on a new urgency among Allied leaders. In light of mounting evidence disclosing the full extent of Nazi atrocities perpetrated under Adolf Hitler, the nature of the crimes cried out for justice. World opinion demanded it.

Conference at Church House

On June 26, 1945, a Four Power delegation representing the United States, Great Britain, France, and the Soviet Union convened at Church House in London to decide on an appropriate Allied response to Nazi war crimes and their perpetrators. This meeting, known as the International Conference on Military Trials, was the first of fifteen sessions held over the ensuing seven weeks to iron out legal procedural problems before bringing formal charges against Nazi war criminals.

14

Robert H. Jackson, the U.S. chief prosecutor, led the way in settling differing viewpoints and arriving at a workable charter for governing the trial to come. Jackson was conservative in appearance—a solid figure in a tailored blue suit with vest and a gold chain arched across the barest hint of a paunch. He exuded the quiet confidence of a man who had risen to a seat on his nation's highest court without benefit of a law degree. He set the agenda, as well as the tone, of the meetings.

The delegation faced a tough task. Although all nations had laws of their own, no laws existed for governing the world at large. The delegates' job would require them to create a world court, empower it, and agree on procedures. And, finally, they would need to develop a statute that would define war crimes and prescribe appropriate punishment for those convicted. Historian Joseph E. Persico describes their task as "the legal equivalent of drafting the Ten Commandments."

Obstacles

The Americans and the British wanted to try accused offenders under the adversarial system of law used in the United States and Britain. Jackson and Britain's attorney general, Sir David Maxwell-Fyfe, whose swarthy complexion, full lips, and deep jowls suggested a Middle Eastern rather than a Scottish heritage, explained the system to the French and Soviet representatives. But both the French and the Soviets preferred the inquisitorial system practiced in Europe in which the judge plays a dominant role and lawyers only help the accused to prepare a case.

In the inquisitorial system the prosecutor assembles all evidence—both for and against the accused person—and presents it to the examining judge. The judge hears all evidence presented, sifts and weighs it, and then decides whether the accused should be brought to trial. If the judge rules in the affirmative, he is effectively finding the person guilty. The burden of proof then shifts to the defendant.

Conversely, the burden of proof rests with the prosecution in the adversarial system of law, which features opposing lawyers, direct examination and cross-examination, and a judge who acts primarily as a referee. After considerable haggling, Jackson and Maxwell-Fyfe persuaded the French and the Soviets to go along with the adversarial system, and the negotiations moved forward.

The chief Soviet negotiator, Major General Ion T. Nikitchenko, a stern, former coal miner with a flat Slavic face and steel-gray eyes, then disagreed with Jackson as to the purpose of the trial. "We are dealing here with the chief war criminals who have already been convicted [in the Soviets' view] and whose conviction has been already announced by both the Moscow and Crimea [Yalta] declarations by the heads of governments." (The Big Three meeting held at Yalta in February 1945 affirmed the Moscow Declaration of November 1943.)

Nikitchenko therefore reasoned that the trial was to be held "only to determine the measure of guilt of each particular person and mete out the necessary punishment—the sentences."

Jackson sharply rejected the concept of predetermined guilt, stating that "if we are going to have a trial, then it must be an actual trial." He felt strongly about preserving the integrity of the trial and using it as an instrument of justice rather than an implement for retribution. Nikitchenko withdrew his argument.

Other potential pitfalls involving anticipated defenses had yet to be examined. What was the court to do, for example, when the accused purported that they were merely following superior orders? Or when they raised a *tu quoque*—"so did you"—defense?

Maxwell-Fyfe warned that a "superior orders" defense would undermine the entire case for the prosecution. Under such a defense, only Hitler could be held responsible for whatever crimes might have been committed—and Hitler was dead. The delegates agreed to consider it only as an aid for establishing degrees of guilt. As for the "so did you" defense—a mockery of justice that implied that since some murderers went free, then all murderers must go free—Jackson flatly dismissed it. The others concurred.

The International Military Tribunal (IMT)

Approximately six weeks after the Four Power representatives had commenced negotiations at Church House, they reached an

Representatives of Britain, America, France, and the Soviet Union meet at the Church House in London to agree on a course of action to bring Nazi war criminals to trial.

accord and adopted a plan similar to the one which U.S. secretary of war Henry L. Stimson had proposed earlier to President Roosevelt.

On August 8 the Four Power nations signed the London Agreement. Stimson's plan had been refined by a team of New York lawyers during the winter of 1944–45. Among other things, the agreement included a charter for an international military tribunal and the procedures it would follow for trying selected, major Nazi war criminals.

The International Military Tribunal, as it was officially named, comprised eight judges—one judge and one alternate from each of the Four Power nations. Under the terms of the earlier Moscow Declaration, defendants would have been tried separately for crimes committed against individual nations. The United States alone held some two hundred thousand prisoners, each potentially subject to a separate trial. If each defendant were to be tried individually by each offended nation, the trials might have taken years. Common sense prevailed at Church House, however, and this approach was abandoned.

The Charges

The tribunal's jurisdiction and governing procedures were set forth in the Charter of the International Military Tribunal. From Article 6 of the charter, criminal charges were drawn up on four counts:

> Count One: Common Plan or Conspiracy; plotting with others to wage wars of aggression in violation of international treaties, agreements, or assurances (as interpreted and determined by the Allies);

> Count Two: Crimes Against Peace; planning, preparation, initiation, and waging wars of aggression;

> Count Three: War Crimes; particularly those crimes involving the maltreatment of prisoners of war in breach of international agreements;

> Count Four: Crimes Against Humanity; such as murder, extermination, enslavement, deportation, and other inhumane acts against civilian populations.

Thus, counts one and two addressed crimes against peace; count three covered war crimes; and count four dealt with crimes against humanity.

During the forthcoming trial the American team would focus on proving charges on count one; the British, on count two; and the Soviet and French teams would assume the burden of proof for counts three and four, respectively, splitting responsibilities for prosecuting crimes committed in eastern and western Europe.

These charges lacked a solid basis in international law and thus evoked immediate and lasting criticism from both lawyers and laypersons. Although conventions at Geneva and The Hague and the Kellogg-Briand Pact of 1928 (which renounced war) had contributed some precedents, the IMT Charter essentially created new laws and applied them ex post facto—after the fact.

Undeniably, the Nazis had initiated an aggressive war and committed unspeakable atrocities. But in the strictest legal sense, although the Nazis had breached many unenforceable treaties and agreements, they had broken no existing laws. In short, the Nazis about to be charged under the IMT Charter

ARTICLE 6 OF THE IMT CHARTER

In establishing the charges by which a handpicked number of Nazi leaders were to be tried at Nuremberg, the IMT's charter embodied unprecedented (and often criticized) legal concepts. Multiple examples of "law after the fact" pervaded the document. Article 6—which defined the charges—stated in part that crimes "for which there will be individual responsibility" are:

(a) CRIMES AGAINST PEACE (the basis for Counts One and Two): namely, planning, preparation, initiation or waging wars of aggression, or a war in violation of international treaties, agreements or assurances, or participation in a common plan or conspiracy for the accomplishment of any of the foregoing;

(b) WAR CRIMES (the basis for Count Three): namely, violations of the laws or customs of war. Such violations shall include, but not be limited to, murder, ill-treatment or deportation to slave labor or for any other purpose of civilian population of or in occupied territory, murder or ill-treatment of prisoners of war or persons on the seas, killing of hostages, plunder of public or private property, wanton destruction of cities, towns or villages, or devastation not justified by military necessity;

(c) CRIMES AGAINST HUMANITY (the basis for Count Four): namely, murder, extermination, enslavement, deportation, and other inhumane acts committed against any civilian population, before or during the war; or persecutions on political, racial or religious grounds in execution of or in connection with any crime within the jurisdiction of the Tribunal, whether or not in violation of the domestic law of the country where perpetrated.

Article 6 concluded with the following admonition:

Leaders, organizers, instigators and accomplices participating in the formulation or execution of a common plan or conspiracy to commit any of the foregoing crimes are responsible for all acts performed by any persons in execution of such plan.

The IMT Charter, flawed, and assembled in great haste, would raise legal, moral, and ethical questions for years to come. In fairness, however, the charter represented an extraordinary effort by a diverse international group willing to concede individual interests and preferences for the good of a common goal.

were to be tried for acts that were not recognized as crimes at the time they committed them.

Jackson took a different view. By establishing a court and defining procedures and punishment, Jackson told the delegates, they were simply supplying a means of enforcing the language of existing treaties:

> Let's not be derailed by legal hair-splitters. Aren't murder, torture, and enslavement crimes recognized by all civilized people? What we propose is to punish acts which have been regarded as criminal since the time of Cain and have been so written in every civilized code.

Notwithstanding the logic of Jackson's impassioned appeal to his fellow jurists, many lawyers continued to find the law controversial, especially count one, the conspiracy charge.

The Conspiracy Concept

Nations had waged war for centuries without ever having been charged with conspiracy. But nations in times past had routinely initiated a war only after issuing a formal declaration. The Nazis had violated this recognized tradition by invading half the countries of Europe without prior warning or declaration of war. For this, the Americans insisted, they deserved to be prosecuted and punished. Count one provided a means to hold both individual Nazis and entire Nazi organizations accountable for their crimes prior to World War II.

The conspiracy concept of two or more parties plotting together to commit an unlawful act was alien to European legal practice. Initially, the French and Soviets argued against the premise, but the Americans eventually convinced them that the only alternative would be to try thousands of Nazis individually. The Americans, with their better understanding of the concept, assumed responsibility for proving conspiracy charges under count one.

The Indictment

On October 6, 1945, four chief prosecutors appointed under the IMT Charter—one from each of the Four Power nations—gathered

International judicial representatives confer during the Nuremberg trials. Included in this photo are Justice Birkett (center, listening to Justice Sir Geoffrey Lawrence). On the far left is General Ion T. Nikitchenko. On the far right is Attorney General Francis Biddle.

in Berlin on a brisk autumn day. Their purpose in the German capital was to sign the indictment—a formal written statement prepared by the prosecutors—charging two dozen handpicked and high-ranking Nazis with war crimes. Each defendant was charged with two or more counts. Fourteen defendants were charged on all four counts.

On October 13 the judges appointed to the International Military Tribunal, including chief U.S. judge Francis Biddle, chose the senior British representative, Lord Justice Sir Geoffrey Lawrence, to preside over the forthcoming trial. The ruddy and round-faced sixty-six-year-old former lord chief justice of Britain was to prove an excellent choice in the long court days ahead. Five days later, on October 18, the judges took their oaths and the court became official.

On that same day, the prosecutors delivered the indictment to the tribunal. The IMT then adjourned and departed for Nuremberg to determine the fate of the twenty-four (later reduced to twenty-two) alleged Nazi war criminals. An outraged world's cries for justice were about to be answered.

Chapter 2

Fate Unfolds

T HE DEFENDANTS, MOST OF WHOM were already imprisoned at the Palace of Justice in Nuremberg, were notified of their indictment on October 19, 1945. They were instructed that they would have thirty days to seek counsel and prepare their defense.

The Indicted

The indicting document listed twenty-four defendants. The list omitted the names of the evilest war criminals of all time: Adolf Hitler, führer of Germany's Third Reich; Heinrich Himmler, leader of the SS (*Schutzstaffel*, or protection squads); and Joseph Goebbels, propaganda minister. Each had taken his own life to avoid prosecution for his crimes.

Of those indicted, Robert Ley, leader of the German labor front, hanged himself in his cell before the proceedings began; and industrialist Gustav Krupp, old and critically ill, was deemed incapable of pleading. Since Martin Bormann, Hitler's secretary, could not be found—either alive or dead—the tribunal directed that he be tried in absentia (in absence).

The list of remaining defendants, by order of indictment, comprised: Hermann Göring, Rudolf Hess, Joachim von Ribbentrop, Wilhelm Keitel, Ernst Kaltenbrunner, Alfred Rosenberg, Hans Frank, Wilhelm Frick, Julius Streicher, Walther Funk, Hjalmar Schacht, Karl Dönitz, Erich Raeder, Baldur von Schirach, Fritz Sauckel, Alfred Jodl, Martin Bormann, Franz von Papen, Artur Seyss-Inquart, Albert Speer, Konstantin von Neurath, and Hans Fritzsche. With regard to their order of indictment and trial appearance, the accused war criminals can be roughly categorized into five groups: the top Nazis, the capital criminals, the bank presidents, and the fleet admirals, leaving nine Nazis that cannot be categorized.

The Top Nazis

Reichsmarschall (Imperial Marshal) Hermann Göring, a former World War I flying ace, had served the Third Reich as commander in chief of the air force (Luftwaffe) and chief of war economy. He held the further distinction of being Adolf Hitler's chosen successor. Hitler once described Göring as "ice cold in times of crisis" and "when it comes to the crunch he's a man of steel—unscrupulous."

During the Nazi reign the pompous, arrogant, and egotistical Göring overindulged himself in the privileges of supreme power and wealth, and his excesses led him on a self-destructive path toward obesity and morphine addiction. When he surrendered himself in the Austrian Alps to the commander of the U.S. 36th Infantry Division on May 7, 1945, Göring carried 246 pounds on his five-foot-six-inch frame.

After his surrender he presented an American general with a photograph of himself, with the inscription: "War is like a football game, whoever loses gives his opponent his hand, and everything is forgiven." Göring would soon discover otherwise. He was indicted on all four counts.

After Göring, Rudolf Hess ranked second in line to succeed Hitler as chancellor of Germany's Third Reich. The black-haired, beetle-browed Hess was one of Hitler's most trusted deputies. In 1923, as a result

Reichsmarschall and commander of the Luftwaffe Hermann Göring greets German airmen during World War II.

Rudolf Hess was indicted at Nuremberg even though he had spent most of the war in a British prison.

of Hitler's failed Munich Beer Hall Putsch (a secret, sudden attempt to over-throw the government), the pair had shared a cell in Landsberg prison, where Hitler dictated most of his autobiography *Mein Kampf (My Struggle)* to his disciple. Hess contributed the con-cept of *Lebensraum* (living space)—the term for Ger-man expansionism—to Hit-ler's renowned text.

Hess earned Hitler's scorn when he flew from Germany to Scotland in May 1941 in an unauthorized attempt to ne-gotiate a peace settlement with the British. Hitler, in-censed, declared Hess insane. The British imprisoned Hess for the war's duration.

Although diagnosed as a psychopath (one with an antisocial mental disorder) and as afflicted with hysterical amnesia (uncon-trollable anxiety accompanied by memory loss), Hess was not considered clinically insane. For his early contributions to the German war effort, he was indicted on all four counts.

The Capital Criminals

As Hitler's adviser in foreign affairs, Joachim von Ribbentrop had effected a successful conclusion to the Anglo-German Naval Treaty in 1935. The pact allowed Germany to increase the size of its surface navy up to 35 percent of the Royal Navy's tonnage, and to build a submarine fleet of 60 to 100 percent equivalency. The boorish—and often bumbling—Ribbentrop took the post of ambassador to Britain the following year. In 1938 Hitler appointed him foreign minister, an office that he held throughout World War II, parroting Hitler's views. For his role as Hitler's spokesperson and in establishing Nazi policy, his indictment specified all four counts.

Field Marshal Wilhelm Keitel, as head of the German Armed Forces High Command, or OKW (Oberkommando der Wehrmacht), from 1938 to 1945, affirmed Germany's unconditional surrender on May 8, 1945. A professional soldier, he had served as an artillery officer on the western front during World War I. After the war he advanced in rank and authority to become second only to Hitler in the military hierarchy. An unabashed admirer of Hitler, Keitel referred to him as "the greatest commander of all time." Hitler called him "loyal as a dog." But his peers, who grew to despise him, contemptuously nicknamed him *Lackeitel* (from *lackei*, "lackey").

As Hitler's senior military adviser throughout the war, the subservient Keitel steadfastly carried out all of Hitler's orders, including one leading to mass executions in Poland. And he tried to justify the massacre of countless Soviet civilians by the *SS Einsatzgruppen* (Special Action Units). Keitel also signed an order encouraging German civilians to lynch captured Allied airmen. For these acts and more, the Allies indicted Keitel on all four counts at Nuremberg.

The scar-faced Ernst Kaltenbrunner, a lawyer, joined the Austrian Nazi Party in 1930 and the Austrian SS in 1933. He headed the organization from 1937 until Germany's annexation of Austria in March 1938. Heinrich Himmler then appointed him *Hoherer SS und Polizeiführer* (higher SS and police leader) in Vienna.

In January 1943 Himmler again elevated the totally loyal Kaltenbrunner to head the Reich Central Security Office (RSHA) of the SS. This command gave Kaltenbrunner complete responsibility for sending millions of Jews and political suspects to their deaths in concentration camps, an assignment he handled with relish. He also authorized the murder of prisoners of war and the shooting of Allied airmen forced to bail out over Germany. Kaltenbrunner, the incarnation of evil, was arraigned on counts one, three, and four.

An Estonian-born member of the Nazi Party, Alfred Rosenberg, aloof and bookish, served as Reich minister of Eastern Occupied Territories. He joined the party in 1920 and began writing anti-Semitic and anti-Christian articles for its newspaper *Völkischer Beobachter* (*Ethnic Observer*). In quick succession he became first the editor and then the managing editor of the newspaper. His volatile racial views contributed greatly to the Nazi doctrine and soon attracted Hitler's attention. Hitler rewarded Rosenberg in 1934 by giving him control of the party's cultural and political policy.

In his *Myth of the 20th Century*, Rosenberg expounded the extremist ethnic theories that he would later implement in eastern Europe. Although he disavowed the Nazis' genocidal practices, he was overruled by more powerful superiors. At Nuremberg, he faced indictment on all four counts.

Hans Frank, who came to be known as "the Jew butcher of Cracow," was another lawyer who had risen to high station within the Nazi Party. He first attracted Hitler's favor in 1927 by defending several storm troopers who had wrecked a restaurant where some Jews were dining. Frank's pro bono defense (Frank donated his services) succeeded in winning light sentences for his clients. Hitler met with Frank after the trial. "You must come and work for the party," Hitler said, refusing to take no for an answer.

Frank's success was assured. He first became Hitler's legal adviser. Then, in quick order, he became Bavaria's minister of justice in 1933, president of the German Law Academy in 1934, and governor-general in Nazi-occupied Poland in 1939. Frank informed the Poles that they would be treated as "slaves of the Greater German Empire" and promptly set about proving it. He inflicted on them the most savage and demeaning practices ever conceived by Nazi policy makers: the Final Solution (the slaughter of six million Jews during the Holocaust); *Lebensborn* (Himmler's plan to accelerate the birthrate of "racially sound" babies, that is, babies of pure Germanic blood); and forced labor. For his zealous implementation of Nazi doctrine, Frank faced indictment on counts one, three, and four at Nuremberg.

Yet another German lawyer and early supporter of the Nazi Party, Wilhelm Frick served as minister of the interior from 1933 until 1943. As minister, he drew up the infamous Nuremberg Laws in 1935, which deprived Jews of German citizenship and many other rights. During his ten-year term in office, he banned trade unionism and freedom of the press. Frick vigorously encouraged anti-Semitism and implemented social measures against Jews (the Final Solution) and the elimination of other enemies of the Nazi regime. Ousted from the minister's post by Himmler in 1943, he was subsequently appointed "Protector" of Bohemia and Moravia. Frick answered a four-count indictment at Nuremberg.

Julius Streicher, who called himself "Jew-baiter number one," established the anti-Semitic German Socialist Party that incorporated into the Nazi Party in 1921. One of the most hated—and certainly one of the most despicable—of all Nazis, he founded the hate-spreading newspaper *Der Stürmer* (*The Stormer*). For more than two decades, Streicher spewed an unrelenting stream of racial prejudice and pure bigotry in the pages of his tabloid. Crude, sadistic, and corrupt, Streicher was so hated by his brethren that, except for the personal protection of Hitler, he might not have survived the war. He faced indictment on counts one and four at Nuremberg.

Julius Streicher awaits trial in his cell at Nuremberg city jail.

The Bank Presidents

As minister of economics and president of the Reichsbank (state bank), Walther Funk played a leading role in planning the economic aspects of Hitler's attack on the

Soviet Union. He later presided over the many personal items that had been stripped from concentration camp victims in occupied territories and deposited in the Reichsbank, such as gold teeth, wedding rings, gold eyeglass rims, and so on. A fat, dumpy, whimpering individual, he disavowed any personal guilt on all four counts of his indictment at Nuremberg.

Hjalmar Schacht, born of Danish descent, was raised in New York as the son of a merchant. He preceded Walther Funk as president of the Reichsbank and served in that capacity from 1923 to 1929. During his presidency he established a new currency that ended Germany's enormous inflation. The Nazis recalled him into service in 1933. The following year, as minister of economics, he restored the German trade balance with innovative methods and an expanding trade policy. He resigned his ministerial post in 1937. Then, as a result of a disagreement with Hitler over rearmament costs, he was dismissed as president of the Reichsbank in 1939.

Grand Admiral Karl Dönitz was indicted at Nuremberg on all four counts.

Schacht later joined the resistance against Hitler and was arrested for high treason after the failed bomb plot on Hitler's life in July 1944. He spent the rest of the war in concentration camps. Nonetheless, Schacht, for his part in financing Germany's rearmament, was indicted on counts one and two.

The Fleet Admirals

A dedicated and gifted naval officer, Grand Admiral Karl Dönitz served first as commander in chief of U-boats, then as commander in chief of the German navy. At war's end Hitler designated him as his successor in place of Göring, and Dönitz became the second and last führer of the Third Reich. He had entered the navy in 1910 and served aboard the cruiser *Breslau* until joining the submarine service in 1916. He became smitten with submarines and was named by Hitler in 1936 to head Germany's U-boat fleet, which Dönitz had developed secretly. Loyal to Hitler till the last, Dönitz ruled over the final days of the Third Reich. The Allies captured him on May 22, 1945, and later indicted him at Nuremberg on all four counts.

Grand Admiral Erich Raeder was appointed commander in chief of the German navy in 1923 and held that position until 1943. During his two decades at the helm, he worked tirelessly—but without a well-thought-out plan—to rebuild the navy and restore Germany as a world-class naval power. Raeder welcomed Hitler's assumption of power, since Hitler had rejected the Versailles settlement (which limited Germany's naval strength) in 1935 and committed Germany to rearmament. But Hitler upset Raeder's timetable in 1939 by entering a war he had assured Raeder would not happen until 1949. Raeder then informed Hitler that his unprepared navy "would only be able to show that they know how to die with honor."

Hitler dismissed Raeder from command in 1943 because of disagreements over naval strategies and objectives. But Raeder's role in preparing Germany for an aggressive war and directing the early aggressions of the German navy was sufficient to warrant his indictment on counts one, two, and three.

The Remaining Nine Nazis

Baldur von Schirach, born in Berlin but three-quarters American, joined the Nazi Party in 1925. In 1932 he became a member of the German Reichstag (parliament), and that same year he founded and organized the Hitler Youth. The son of a former director of the National Theater in Weimar, Schirach built a close-knit, strictly disciplined society of young people that eventually numbered some nine million German boys and girls. Their curriculum supposedly instructed them in matters of health, beauty, and culture but instead indoctrinated them in the fascist Nazi philosophy and prepared them for war. Schirach, who likened himself to a scout leader, enjoyed saying, "Every German boy who dies at the front is dying for Mozart."

Schirach directed the German youth movement until his appointment as *gauleiter* (political district leader) of Vienna in 1940. As *gauleiter* he sent Jews by the tens of thousands to their deaths in the concentration camp at Auschwitz, Poland. Schirach answered to charges on counts one and four at Nuremberg.

Fritz Sauckel headed the German conscript labor organization. As its director he drafted more than five million workers from occupied countries into his workforce. A Nazi Party member from 1923, he had risen to high office through successive appointments in Thuringia in central Germany. He became its *gauleiter* in 1927, its minister president in 1932, and then its governor. In 1942 Hitler selected him to direct the mobilization of Germany's entire workforce, including foreigners and prisoners of war. Sauckel's enslavement and inhuman treatment of foreign workers, in violation of the laws of war, led to his indictment on all four counts at Nuremberg.

One of Hitler's closest military advisers, General Alfred Jodl served as chief of the operations staff of the German Armed Forces High Command (OKW). Jodl had gained much frontline experience as an officer in World War I before joining the general staff as a captain in 1919. He met Hitler in 1923 and quickly became a devotee of his future führer. Jodl rose to the rank of general of artillery in 1939 and was appointed OKW operations chief in 1939, a position that he held throughout the war.

Working immediately under Hitler and his father-in-law, Wilhelm Keitel, Jodl directed every German campaign of the war except for Operation Barbarossa (the invasion of the USSR). Only Keitel exceeded Jodl's loyalty to the führer. Jodl sat before the IMT charged with a four-count indictment.

Martin Bormann, a crude, crass ex-convict, imprisoned in 1924 for taking part in a murder, joined the Nazi Party upon his release in 1925. Elected as his party's representative to the Reichstag in 1933, he also served as Rudolf Hess's private secretary and right-

THE NUREMBERG LAWS

From the time Hitler became Germany's chancellor in 1933, until he launched his blitzkrieg against Poland in 1939, Hitler flouted the laws of human decency within Germany. He constructed concentration camps and imprisoned communists and other political opponents. He imposed Nazi Party control over labor unions, professional associations, and business organizations. And he nullified the existing legal system and appointed himself as Supreme Judge with the power to imprison or execute individuals without benefit of trial.

Of great future significance to the Nuremberg trials, he enacted a series of laws progressively outlawing Jews from all positions of private or public authority. He denied them the rights of German citizenship. And he criminalized marriage or sexual intimacy between Jews and German citizens.

Hitler's first two anti-Semitic laws are identified by the place and date of their enactment, that is, as the Nuremberg Laws of 1935.

hand man from then until 1941. Bormann then endeared himself to Hitler and was made head of the party chancellery. In 1943 he effectively replaced Hess as Hitler's private secretary.

Working quietly behind the scenes of power politics, skillfully fostering intrigue and relentlessly increasing his influence, Bormann emerged as perhaps the second most powerful Nazi next to Hitler himself in the last days of the Third Reich. On May 1, 1945—the day after Hitler's suicide—Bormann left Hitler's bunker in Berlin and disappeared mysteriously. He was indicted in absentia on all four counts at Nuremberg.

Franz von Papen, as chancellor of Germany from June to November 1932, worked toward Hitler's accession to that position in January 1933. He then became vice chancellor under Hitler and later served as ambassador to Austria (1936–38) and Turkey (1939–44). Perhaps one of his obituaries best documents his chief claim to fame: "Franz von Papen will be remembered as the man who held his hands for Hitler to jump into the saddle." The IMT indictment charged him on counts one and two.

Artur Seyss-Inquart, the son of a Moravian schoolteacher, took a law degree at Vienna University in 1931, after which he joined the Nazi Party. He then served as an Austrian state councillor until appointed—after pressure from Hitler—Austrian minister of the interior in 1938. This afforded him control of the country's internal security, as well as its police force, allowing him to play a key role in Germany's annexation of Austria in March 1938.

Hitler moved Seyss-Inquart to the occupied Netherlands in 1940, where he served as Reich commissioner until the end of the war. As commissioner he oversaw the deportation of some 140,000 Dutch Jews to concentration camps, where about 117,000 of them were slain. The outwardly pleasant, extremely intelligent Seyss-Inquart faced indictment at Nuremberg on all four counts.

An architect by profession, Albert Speer joined the Nazi Party in 1931 and became Hitler's chief architect in 1933. His early credits included the arrangement of the 1934 Nuremberg rally, a massive demonstration in support of Hitler and the Nazi Party, and the design of the Reichschancellery, seat of the Nazi

Artur Seyss-Inquart was indicted on all four counts at Nuremberg.

Although architect Albert Speer (right) claimed to be ignorant of the crimes committed against the Jews and turned against Hitler in the final months of the war, he was indicted on all four counts at Nuremberg.

government in Berlin. He served as minister for armaments and munitions from 1942 to 1945 and was given full responsibility for the direction of Germany's economy in 1945. Speer turned against Hitler in the final months of the war and later claimed ignorance of Nazi war crimes. At Nuremberg, Speer faced indictment on all four counts.

Baron Konstantin von Neurath, a career diplomat, served as foreign minister from 1932 to 1938. He was retained by Hitler to help gain the free world's acceptance of the Nazis' ascendancy to power in 1933 and partly to shroud the dramatic changes occurring within Germany. When it became no longer necessary to conceal Nazi aims and activities from the outside world, Hitler replaced Neurath with Ribbentrop. In 1939 Neurath was appointed Reich protector of the Czech territories, serving until replaced by Reinhard Heydrich—the notorious Nazi "hangman"—in 1943. Neurath was indicted on all four counts at Nuremberg.

Hans Fritzsche, the last of the twenty-two Nazis to face charges at Nuremberg, was a minor official relative to the others. As a civilian he had enjoyed a career as a popular radio commentator. His radio expertise, and a voice that greatly resembled that of Goebbels, led to his appointment as chief of radio operations in the Nazi propaganda ministry. Prior to the Nuremberg trial, he had never met most of his codefendants. Although he stubbornly disclaimed any knowledge of Nazi wrongdoing, Fritzsche answered to indictment on counts one, three, and four.

Every one of the defendants denied his guilt, deferring blame for his predicament to the dead Himmler, the missing Bormann, and one or two others.

Anticipation

On the morning of November 20, 1945, journalists from twenty-three nations jammed into 250 maroon-cushioned tilt-up seats in Room 600 of Nuremberg's Palace of Justice. In the gallery above, additional spectators filled 150 similar seats. Thick, sound-muffling carpeting and dark-paneled walls hung with heavy sage green drapes contributed to a courtroom aura of what Justice Jackson described as "melancholy grandeur."

Shortly before 10 A.M., a small sliding door in the rear of the prisoners' dock opened and the din of excited conversation faded abruptly into a breathless hush. Nineteen defendants filed uncertainly into the prisoners' dock, blinking in the glare of the harsh fluorescent lights. They seated themselves quietly. Göring scowled defiantly. Hess looked dazed. Ribbentrop appeared drained of emotion. All faced the court and waited in uneasy anticipation for their fate to unfold.

Chapter 3

The Anglo-American Prosecution

A MINUTE OR SO BEFORE 10 A.M., marshal of the court Colonel Charles W. Mayes, in a booming voice commanded, "Atten-shun! All rise. The tribunal will now enter!" A small door opened and the judges filed in and took their places on the bench. The American and British judges wore plain black robes. White bibs and ruffled wrists and a touch of ermine adorned the robes of the two French judges. The two Soviet judges, garbed in chocolate uniforms with green trim and gold shoulderboards, imparted color and infused the bench with a sense of its military birthright and purpose.

At precisely 10 A.M. on this morning of November 20, 1945, Lord Chief Justice Sir Geoffrey Lawrence rapped his gavel and said, "This trial, which is now to begin, is unique in the annals of history." He then announced that the proceedings would begin with the reading of the indictment.

Day of Atonement

Prosecutors alternated reading the long, often boring document and its three appendages. Under the heat of the high-powered lights, installed for the benefit of motion picture cameras that were positioned to film every minute of the entire trial, several of the defendants fell asleep in the dock and had to be prodded awake by the courtroom guards. But not all of the reading was boring.

An overall view of the courtroom in Nuremberg. The indicted Nazis sit on the far right.

A young French lawyer and survivor of a Nazi concentration camp captured the attention of several of the defendants when he read:

> Out of a convoy of 230 French women deported from Compiègne to Auschwitz in January 1943, 180 were worked to death within four months. Over 780 French priests were executed at Mauthausen.

In the dock Field Marshal Wilhelm Keitel, chief of staff of the German armed forces, bowed his head. Nazi foreign minister Joachim von Ribbentrop dabbed continuously at a sweating forehead. Walther Funk, president of the Reichsbank sobbed quietly. The imperious Hermann Göring studiously kept a record of how many times the names of each defendant was mentioned. His name led the others by a wide margin.

After two and a half hours, the court recessed for lunch. The defendants ate in the courtroom that day. They would eat on the top floor of the Palace of Justice for the rest of the trial. Lunch afforded the defendants an opportunity to chat and exchange opinions. Some of them had not met before. Others like Funk and Göring, Dönitz and Speer, and Jodl and Keitel were acquaintances of long standing.

Personal enmities pervaded the diverse group. Göring, Papen, and Neurath barely spoke to one another. No one spoke to Streicher, who despised Göring, who hated Schacht. Ribbentrop was equally detested by Rosenberg, Papen, Neurath, and Göring. Speer was marginally acceptable to Göring and Sauckel. Raeder looked at Dönitz as a brash subordinate and blamed Germany's loss of the war on the incompetence of Göring and Keitel.

Ironically, the one person who seemed acceptable to all the defendants was the American prison psychologist, Captain Gustav M. Gilbert, who regularly joined them for lunch. Ribbentrop asked Gilbert:

> Why all the fuss about breaking treaties? Did you ever read about the history of the British Empire? Why, it's full of broken treaties, oppression of minorities, mass murder, aggressive wars, and everything.

The foreign minister spoke the truth, but as Gilbert encouraged him to admit, past crimes scarcely represent an acceptable pattern for international law.

During lunch several of the defendants commented that the food was getting better. Baldur von Schirach, head of the Hitler Youth, commented with a grin to Gilbert, "I suppose we will get steak the day you hang us." The reading of counts three and four commenced after lunch, followed by the reading of charges against the individual defendants, which carried over to the next morning.

The day-and-a-half-long reading of the indictment made it clear that much of the prosecution's case would be directed toward Nazi crimes against forced laborers and prisoners of war and toward crimes against the Jews during the so-called Holocaust. Some six million Jews had perished as victims of the Nazis' Final Solution to the "Jewish problem," along with countless numbers of communists, homosexuals, Gypsies, and blacks.

For the Nazis in the prisoners' dock, the day of atonement for their crimes had at last arrived.

"History Will Judge Us Tomorrow"

On November 21, after each of the defendants had pleaded not guilty to the charges, Lawrence called upon "the Chief Prosecutor of the United States," Robert Jackson. The fifty-three-year-old Jackson, impeccably attired in a white shirt, tie, and conservative dark blue suit, accented by a white handkerchief and his habitual gold chain, rose and stood before the International Military Tribunal. Speaking with restrained emotion to the court and to the motion picture cameras, he delivered a forceful opening address that rang with eloquence and perception:

> The privilege of opening the first trial in history for crimes against the peace of the world imposes a grave responsibility. The wrongs which we seek to condemn and punish have been so calculated, so malignant, and so devastating, that civilization cannot tolerate their being ignored, because it cannot survive their being repeated. That four great nations, flushed with victory and stung with injury, stay the hand of vengeance and voluntarily submit their captive enemies to the judgment of the law is one of the most significant tributes that Power has ever paid to reason.

Jackson immediately dismissed the notion of "victors' justice." He pointed out that "the nature of these crimes is such that both the prosecution and judgment must be by victor nations over vanquished foes." But he cautioned that "we must never forget that the record on which we judge these defendants is the record on which history will judge us tomorrow."

"To Live by No Man's Leave"

The charismatic prosecutor continued, touching succinctly on Nazi excesses and abuses: He cataloged the wholesale arrests of opponents of the Nazi regime; the advent of concentration camps; and the outlawing of Jewry, which led ultimately to the attempted annihilation of an entire race of people—the Holocaust.

Jackson devoted the last part of his address to legal issues, justifying why aggressive war should be treated as a crime; why government officials should be held personally liable; why the defense of "only following orders" constitutes an invalid defense; and explaining the rationale for indicting the chief Nazi agencies and the German Armed Forces High Command as criminal organizations. He concluded his moving monologue with an appeal to the tribunal for justice:

> Civilization asks whether law is so laggard as to be utterly helpless to deal with crimes of this magnitude by criminals of this order of importance. It does not expect that you [the tribunal] can make war impossible. It does expect that your juridical action will put the forms of international law, its precepts, its prohibitions and, most of all, its sanctions, on the side of peace, so that men and women of good will, in all countries, may have "leave to live by no man's leave, underneath the law."

The tribunal adjourned after Jackson's introductory discourse, and Jackson and his colleagues spent the evening troubling over eleventh-hour preparations for the greatest trial of their lives.

"A Good Afternoon"

The Allies had assembled a contingent of twenty-three U.S. attorneys under Justice Robert H. Jackson, seven British barristers directed by Sir David Maxwell-Fyfe and British attorney general Sir Hartley Shawcross, five French advocates, and eleven Soviet lawyers. The Americans, charged with prosecuting count one of the indictment, led off the lengthy proceedings that would eventually require four hundred open sessions of court. During these sessions, every word spoken would be translated into English, German, French, and Russian.

In making their case based on count one, conspiracy to wage aggressive (undeclared) war, the American team traced the history of the Nazi movement through the use of captured German documents. The incriminating documents centered on early

Sir David Maxwell-Fyfe, British prosecutor, and Justice Robert H. Jackson, U.S. prosecutor, at a press conference. Jackson set the tone of the trials, insisting on written evidence over eyewitness testimony.

Nazi aggressions against Austria, Czechoslovakia, and Poland. Justice Jackson had insisted earlier that there was "no count in the indictment that can't be proved by books and records."

Jackson preferred to rely on irrefutable written evidence rather than risk the unreliability of witnesses, who were subject to falsifying testimony, memory lapses, and playing to the court and courtroom audience to enhance their own interests. This strategy, although highly effective, was to prove equally boring.

On November 29, sensing the need to enliven the proceedings, navy commander James Donovan approached the prosecutor's lectern and said:

> May it please the tribunal, I refer to document number 2430 PS, a motion picture entitled "Nazi Concentration Camps," which the United States now offers into evidence. It was compiled from motion pictures taken by Allied military photographers as the armies in the West liberated areas in which these camps were located.

The courtroom darkened, except for the prisoners' dock, which remained lighted for security reasons, and a cone of light pierced the dark and projected flickering images of Nazi evil upon a screen on the back wall behind the witness box.

Captain Gilbert noted the reactions of the defendants. Some of his notes are shown here:

> Fritzsche [chief of radio operations in the propaganda ministry] . . . already looks pale and sits aghast as it starts with scenes of prisoners burned alive in a barn. . . . Frick shakes head at illustration of "violent death"—Frank mutters "Horrible!". . . . Defense attorneys are now muttering, "for God's sake—terrible." Sauckel [head of conscript labor movement] shudders at pictures of Buchenwald crematorium oven. . . . [A]s human skin lampshade is shown, Streicher says, "I don't believe that.". . . Frank nods his head bitterly and says, "Horrible!". . . Ribbentrop looks up at screen as British officer starts to speak, saying he has already buried 17,000 corpses. . . . Frick shakes his head incredulously at speech of female doctor describing treatment and experiments on female prisoners at Belsen. . . . Funk crying bitterly, claps hand over mouth as women's naked corpses are thrown into pit. . . . Keitel and Ribbentrop look up at mention of tractor clearing corpses, see it, then hang their heads. . . . Streicher shows signs of disturbance for the first time. . . . Film ends.

Gilbert further noted that after the showing of the film, Streicher said something about "perhaps in the last days." Fritzsche replied derisively, "Millions? In the last days?—No." A subdued Göring shook his head and said, "It was such a good afternoon, too—and then they showed that awful film, and it just spoiled everything."

Talk of Honor

Although the graphic film maligned the defendants as a group, it established little in the way of individual guilt. But the next day, testimony offered by Major General Erwin Lahousen, ranking survivor of the Abwehr, the Nazi counterintelligence agency, directly targeted Keitel and Ribbentrop.

Lahousen, a tall, hollow-eyed walking cadaver, a man totally broken in spirit, walked stiltlike to the stand. Jackson hoped that Lahousen's testimony would add a human dimension and heighten interest in his thus far drab presentation. Colonel John H. Amen, Jackson's chief of interrogation, conducted the examination. The most damaging part of Lahousen's testimony concerned a series of meetings he had attended with Keitel and Ribbentrop in Poland in September 1939, shortly before Poland's collapse.

He testified about Keitel and Ribbentrop's knowledge of, and involvement in, what Hitler termed "political housekeeping," in Poland. The "housekeeping" chores consisted of exterminating "the Polish intelligentsia, the nobility, the clergy, and, of course, the Jews." Keitel, according to Lahousen's testimony, had also ordered the (failed) assassinations of two French generals (who later became leaders in the French resistance). Keitel was heard to say, "I was only doing my duty and following orders."

Lahousen went on to describe a murderous Nazi policy toward Soviet captives who "could be identified as thoroughly bolshevized or as active representatives of the Bolshevist ideology."

During lunch, according to Captain Gilbert, Göring fumed and denounced Lahousen. "That traitor! That's one we forgot on the 20th of July!" Göring was referring to the purge and execution of those who participated in the failed bomb plot on Hitler's life. Göring further spewed:

> Hitler was right—the Abwehr was a traitor's organization! [Admiral Walter Wilhelm Canaris, the Abwehr's head, had provoked Hitler's ire by trying to forestall Hitler's plans for an aggressive war.] How do you like that! No wonder we lost the war—our own Intelligence Service was sold out to the enemy! . . . What good is the testimony of a traitor? He should have been busy giving me accurate results of our bombing missions instead of sabotaging our war efforts. Now I know why I could never depend on him for

accurate information. Just wait till I ask him that one question, 'Why did you not renounce your position, if you were convinced a German victory would be a tragedy?" Just wait till I get a chance at him.

The scholarly General Alfred Jodl, operations chief of the German army, accepted Lahousen's testimony more philosophically:

If he was convinced of it, all well and good, but then he should have said something, and not betrayed his officer's honor. I know they are always asking me what I would have done if I had known of Hitler's plans. I would have said something, but I wouldn't have acted dishonorably.

When Gilbert observed that there seemingly had been a struggle between conscience and duty, and Lahousen had followed his conscience, Jodl replied, "Oh, but you can't do such things. An officer must follow orders or resign." Keitel agreed, but he seemed more concerned about Lahousen's damaging testimony.

General Alfred Jodl defended his colleagues' actions during the war, claiming that it would be dishonorable to disobey orders.

"That man was just reading from a prepared script!" Keitel complained. "I'm going to tell my lawyer." Gilbert said that he didn't think Lahousen had read from a prepared script but that the issue was a question of the truth of the testimony. Keitel then "fell back on the 'officer's honor' argument, without making much sense." Later, Lahousen remarked to Gilbert:

> Now they talk of honor, after millions have been murdered! No doubt it's unpleasant for them to have some one [sic] who can stand up and state these uncomfortable truths to their faces.—I've got to speak for those whom they murdered.—I am the only one left.

Lahousen appeared for cross-examination that afternoon, affording the prosecution its first chance to see the German defense team conduct a cross-examination.

No Help at All

In attempting to rebut or minimize Lahousen's testimony, German defense lawyers demonstrated their unfamiliarity with the process of cross-examination, which is not used in the German (inquisitorial) system of law. As might be expected, the lawyers for Keitel and Ribbentrop engaged Lahousen for the longest time.

Dr. Otto Nelte, representing Keitel, fell into a beginner's trap of asking long, convoluted questions. Nelte's complex questions either failed to keep the witness focused on a single point or raised new issues that invited his unfavorable replies. In one instance, Nelte encouraged Lahousen to say that Keitel had never issued political rather than military instructions to his staff. The gaunt Lahousen answered that Keitel had made it clear that only dedicated Nazi officers were welcome at OKW staff meetings.

Dr. Fritz Sauter, counsel for Ribbentrop, Funk, and Schirach, asking even longer questions, made little headway in an attempt to discredit Lahousen.

> **Sauter:** Witness, your memory deceives you, because immediately after Hitler's attack on Austria you called on the general staff in Berlin and there you tried to get a

commission in the German Wehrmacht, and you now deny this. You also filled in and signed a questionnaire in which you declared your complete allegiance to the Greater German Reich, and to Adolf Hitler; and shortly afterward you took the oath of allegiance to Adolf Hitler.

Lahousen: I can easily explain why my rise in office was so rapid. [As an Austrian military intelligence officer, my efforts were specifically] directed against the neighboring country of Czechoslovakia. Czechoslovakia was the country that was next on the list after Austria. Therefore, it was natural that my later chief, Canaris, was very interested in having me promoted in his department.

Sauter: Then it is true you did go to Berlin and apply to be transferred into the German Wehrmacht, which you at first denied?

Lahousen: No, that is not true, I did not apply. Others made the request. I can even say that I did not *go* there, I *flew* there! [Emphasis added.]

Justice Biddle cocked his eyebrow at Lahousen's final comment. A subsequent consensus indicated that the German lawyers had failed to help their clients.

The British Case

On Tuesday morning, December 4, 1945, the Americans deferred their presentation of evidence to allow the British to open their case based on count-two charges (crimes against peace). British chief prosecutor Sir Hartley Shawcross, well groomed and as handsome as a movie star, struck a stately figure as he stood at the podium and delivered an opening address rivaling Jackson's in eloquence.

Much like the Americans before him, Sir Hartley read from and commented on confiscated German documents that illustrated how the Nazis had planned and waged aggressive wars. Confining himself to highlights of the most striking parts of the documents, he quickly covered the Nazi invasions of Poland,

Denmark, Norway, Belgium, the Netherlands, Greece, Yugoslavia, and the Soviet Union. A typical example of the documents read by Sir Hartley was a report written by Hermann Graebe, a German construction official at a plant in Nazi-occupied Ukraine. Graebe described what he had seen while watching a German SS unit herding thousands of Jews out of the town of Dubno to an earth embankment outside the city:

> Without screaming or weeping, these people undressed, stood around in family groups, kissed each other, said farewells. . . . An old woman with snow-white hair was holding a one-year-old child in her arms and singing to it and tickling it. The child was cooing with delight. . . . A father was holding the hand of a boy about ten years old and speaking to him softly; the boy was fighting back his tears.

One of the SS men counted off twenty persons, by then naked, and sent them behind the earth mound. Graebe moved behind the mound and saw a pit

> already two-thirds full. . . . They went down into the pit, lined themselves up against the previous victims and were shot. . . . I well remember a girl, slim, with black hair, who, as she passed close to me pointed to herself and said, "Twenty-three years old.". . . . I looked for the man who did the shooting; he was an SS man, who sat at the narrow end of the pit, his feet dangling into it. He had a tommy-gun on his knees and was smoking a cigarette.

The smoker, and others like him, thus eliminated the five thousand Jews of Dubno in a single day.

Sir Hartley concluded his opening remarks, calling on the tribunal to punish the defendants for their crimes "so that the world will see the consequences of such conduct and the end to which it must inevitably lead."

Sir David Maxwell-Fyfe, the de facto (actual) head of the British prosecution (under the nominal direction of Sir Hartley), then replaced Sir Hartley at the lectern and informed the tribunal that his team would not call witnesses but instead would

Jewish prisoners are taken by boxcar to concentration camps. Many eyewitnesses provided testimony at Nuremberg to prove the crimes against humanity committed by the Nazis.

rely on documentary evidence. A succession of young lawyers followed Maxwell-Fyfe at the lectern. They introduced voluminous documentation (but none more poignant that Graebe's report) describing Nazi aggressions ranging from Norway to Greece to the Soviet Union.

The British case, built on documentary evidence from German files, strongly implicated Keitel, Ribbentrop, Rosenberg, Raeder, and Jodl as planners and perpetrators of aggressive actions. It also implicated Göring and Dönitz, but to a lesser degree. Maxwell-Fyfe's team presented their portion of the prosecution's case clearly and quickly, using less than four days of court time. Afterward, Göring told Captain Gilbert:

> I still can't grasp all those things. Do you suppose that I'd have believed it if somebody came to me and said they were making freezing experiments on human guinea pigs—or that people were forced to dig their own graves and were mowed down by the thousands? I would just have said, "Get the hell out of here with that fantastic nonsense!"

Gilbert learned later that Göring had advised the prison chaplain that he would attend church that evening.

A Magnetic Personality

On December 11 U.S. assistant prosecutor James Donovan offered in evidence a film entitled *The Nazi Plan* and informed the tribunal that "it sums up the case thus far presented under Counts One and Two of the Indictment." The film offered little in the way of new evidence, but it showed many of the defendants in their old roles and in groups. It was hoped that the film would help the tribunal to form clearer mental images of the alleged conspirators. A few of those conspirators surprised everyone with their reactions to the film. Raeder's defense counsel, Dr. Victor von der Lippe, wrote in his diary:

> Göring was visibly delighted to see himself once more "in the good old times," Ribbentrop spoke of the gripping force of Hitler's personality, another defendant declared himself happy that the Tribunal would see him at least once in full uniform, and with the dignity of his office.

That evening in his cell, Ribbentrop confessed to Captain Gilbert that he would still follow Hitler's orders. "Isn't it amazing? Can't you really feel the terrific magnetism of his personality?"

The Nazi Organizations

The remainder of the American case concentrated on completing the conspiracy charges and on demonstrating the guilt of seven Nazi organizations indicted under Article 9 of the IMT Charter: the Reich Cabinet, the Political Leadership Corps, the SS (protection squads), the SD (security service), the SA (storm troopers or Brownshirts), the OKW (German High Command), and the Gestapo (state secret police). If the organizations could be proved criminal, their members would accordingly be subject to guilt by association and subsequent prosecution.

The presentation of the remaining documentary evidence, which followed the established, often wearisome pattern, was

SHOCKING EVIDENCE

On December 11, 1945, after the incriminating film *The Nazi Plan* had been entered into evidence and shown to the court, U.S. assistant prosecutor Major William F. Walsh shocked the courtroom with documented evidence of the Nazis' persecution of Jews. His grisly inventory included a copy of an address made by Hans Frank to a group of German officials at Kraków in December 1941, in which he said:

> As far as the Jews are concerned, I want to tell you quite frankly that they must be done away with one way or another. . . . We will principally have pity on the German people only and nobody else in the whole world. . . . Gentlemen, I must ask you to arm yourself against all feeling of pity. We must annihilate the Jews, wherever it is possible, in order to maintain the structure of the Reich as a whole.

Walsh read from SS General Jürgen Stroop's report of the razing of the Warsaw ghetto. He presented documents that told of SS gas extermination vans and of how gold had been extracted from the teeth of Jewish victims. According to Hoettl, another two million Jews had been killed by the Einsatzgruppen (mobile killing squads) and other SS agencies.

This revelation appalled Admiral Raeder's defense counsel, Dr. Victor von der Lippe, who noted in his diary:

> No words can express the brutality, cynicism, and villainy of these ideas of Hitler, Himmler, and their agents and helpers! "Outrageous" is too weak, "devilish" and "satanic" are more like it. It is contemptible that Stroop should call his operation a "battle" although the SS suffered 16 "casualties," while 65,000 Jews were "destroyed."

Captain Samuel Harris followed Walsh to the lectern and documented Nazi policies of Germanization (extermination or expulsion of "undesirables") and looting in Nazi-occupied countries. He read from captured copies of two of Himmler's speeches. Himmler spoke of hauling away a hundred thousand Poles in temperatures forty degrees below zero, and of shooting thousands of Polish leaders.

The Americans presented enough documentary evidence at Nuremberg to prove the charges against most of the defendants a thousand times over.

---

interrupted at the close of the court day on December 20, when the tribunal adjourned for the holidays. Court resumed on January 2, 1946. Assistant chief prosecutor Telford Taylor concluded his prosecution of the Nazi organizations on January 7, which effectively completed the core of the American case. British and

Joachim von Ribbentrop (right) leans in front of Rudolf Hess to confer with his lawyer while Hermann Göring (center) smiles and talks to Karl Dönitz (rear right). Göring's jovial behavior at the trials angered those in attendance.

American prosecutors then directed a final barrage of damning documents and testimony against individual defendants over the next several days. They ended their case on January 16.

The world then looked ahead with interest to the French-Soviet prosecution based on counts three and four of the indictment. The tribunal, by then wearying and showing signs of boredom, faced the new phase of the trial with mixed feelings.

Chapter 4

The French-Soviet Prosecution

ALTHOUGH THE FRENCH AND THE SOVIETS shared responsibility for prosecuting both count three (war crimes) and count four (crimes against humanity) of the charter, the enormity of evidence already presented by the British and American prosecutors was more than sufficient to convict most of the defendants. But the French and Soviets—whose lands, unlike those of the British and Americans, had been invaded, occupied, and pillaged by the Nazis—deserved their day in court.

The French Case

On January 17, 1946, forty-five-year-old former French resistance fighter François de Menthon, chief prosecutor for the Republic of France, opened the French case for the prosecution. In his opening remarks, de Menthon viewed the Nazi regime as "a sin against the spirit" and sought the judgment of the court so that National Socialism would be "inscribed permanently as the crime of crimes which could lead only to material and moral perdition."

The French case centered on Nazi barbarism in the concentration camps, where human beings had been dehumanized and reduced to a tattooed number, a nonentity to be used for whatever purpose the wickedest mind could imagine.

Maurice Lampe, a prisoner at the Mauthausen camp in Austria, offered particularly distressing testimony about forty-seven downed American, British, and Dutch airmen who were sent to

Mauthausen to be executed, apparently for no greater crime than attempting to escape capture:

> I must mention that one of the American officers asked the commander that he be allowed to meet his death as a soldier. In reply he was bashed with a whip. The 47 were led barefoot to the quarry.

> For all the prisoners at Mauthausen the murder of these men has remained in their minds like a scene from Dante's *Inferno*. This is how it was done: At the bottom of the steps they loaded stones on the backs of these poor men and they had to carry them to the top. The first journey was made with stones weighing 25 to 30 kilos [55 to 66 pounds] and was accompanied by blows. Then they were made to run down. For the second journey the stones were still heavier; and when the poor wretches sank under their burden, they were kicked and hit with a bludgeon, even stones were hurled at them.

> This went on for several days. In the evening when I returned from the gang with which I was working, the road which led to the camp was a bath of blood. I almost stepped on the lower jaw of a man. Twenty-one bodies were strewn along the road. Twenty-one had died on the first day. The twenty-six others died the following morning.

Frenchman Maurice Lampe, a former inmate of the Mauthausen extermination camp, tells the Nuremberg tribunal how Himmler visited the camp in 1944 to personally attend to the execution and cremation of fifty Soviet officers.

Not a single defense attorney opted to cross-examine Lampe.

French deputy chief prosecutor Charles Debost, bald, with glasses and an air of profound seriousness, questioned a second camp inmate, François Boix. Boix, a professional photographer, had survived Mauthausen because of his usefulness to the Nazis:

Debost: Did you ever see any defendant in the dock at Mauthausen?

Boix: Speer.

Debost: When did you see him?

Boix: In 1943. I did not see him myself, but the head of the identification department took a roll of film with his Leica, which I developed. I recognized Speer and some SS leaders.

Debost: You saw Speer in the pictures you developed?

Boix: Yes. Afterward, I had to write his name and the date on the print.

In all, recalled the lank and intense Boix, there were thirty-six pictures of Speer, some of which showed him shaking hands with Franz Ziereis, the commandant of Mauthausen.

When Boix finished, the prosecution read minutes from a meeting of the Central Planning Board, revealing that Speer had declared, "There is nothing to be said against the SS taking drastic steps and putting known slackers in concentration camps. There is no alternative." A memo from the files of the SS was next read into the record, stating, "Albert Speer has been enrolled as an SS man on my staff by my order," signed "Heinrich Himmler, *Reichsführer*." In the dock, Speer shifted uneasily.

Ordinary People

On January 28, one of Debost's more memorable witnesses took the stand to testify about her experiences in Auschwitz. Thirty-three-year-old Marie Claude Vaillant-Couturier (appropriately, "valiant dressmaker" in English), an anti-Fascist journalist when France fell, had been sent to the dreaded concentration camp for refusing to sign a false confession. Appearing in a tailored blue suit, with her hair combed back tightly and her face free of makeup, she emanated dignity. In a steady voice, she told the court that she had been assigned to a sewing block at the camp.

> We lived right where the trains stopped. They ran practically right up to the gas chamber. Consequently, we saw the unsealing of the cars and the soldiers letting men, women, and children out. We saw old couples forced to part from each other, mothers forced to abandon their young children. All of these people were unaware of the fate awaiting them. To make their arrival more pleasant, an orchestra composed of pretty girls in white blouses and navy blue skirts played during the selection process, gay tunes from *The Merry Widow* and *The Tales of Hoffmann*. Those selected for the gas chamber, old people, mothers, and small children, were escorted immediately to a red brick building.

> All my life, I will remember Annette Epaux. I saw her on a truck that was taking people to the gas chamber. She had her arms around another French woman. When the truck started she called to me, "Think of my little boy, if you ever get back to France." Then they began singing the "Marseillaise" [France's national anthem].

Madame Marie Claude Vaillant-Couturier gives the Nuremberg tribunal a horrifying account of her two and a half years in Nazi concentration camps.

SYNONYM FOR HORROR

During the French case for the prosecution, Marie Claude Vaillant-Couturier, an Auschwitz survivor, testified about her experiences as an inmate of the dreaded labor camp. She had been sent to the camp in January 1943 in a convoy of 230 French women, of whom only 49 returned alive. Vaillant-Couturier described their journey to, and arrival at, Auschwitz this way:

> It was a terrible journey. We were 60 in a car and we were given no food or drink during the journey. At the various stopping places we asked the Lorraine soldiers of the Wehrmacht who were guarding us whether we would arrive soon; and they replied, "If you knew where you are going you would not be in a hurry to get there."

> We arrived at Auschwitz at dawn. The seals on our cars were broken and we were driven out by blows with the butt end of a rifle, and taken to the Birkenau Camp, a section of the Auschwitz Camp. It is situated in the middle of a great plain, which was frozen in the month of January. During this part of the journey we had to drag our luggage. As we passed through the door we knew only too well how slender our chances were that we would come out again, for we had already met columns of living skeletons going to work; as we entered we sang "The Marseillaise" [the French national anthem] to keep up our courage.

> We were led to a large shed, then to the disinfecting station. There our heads were shaved and our registration numbers were tattooed on the left forearm. Then we were taken into a large room for a steam bath and a cold shower. In spite of the fact that we were all naked, all this took place in the presence of SS men and women. We were then given clothing which was soiled and torn, a cotton dress and jacket of the same material.

> As all this had taken several hours, we saw from the windows of the block where we were, the camp of the men; and toward the evening an orchestra came in. It was snowing and we wondered why they were playing music. We then saw that the camp foremen were returning to the camp. Each foreman was followed by men who were carrying the dead. As they could hardly drag themselves along, every time they stumbled, they were put on their feet again by being kicked or by blows with the butt end of a rifle.

By the end of the day, Vaillant-Couturier and her companions had discovered why the camp at Auschwitz had become widely known as a synonym for horror.

> One night, we were awakened by horrible cries. The
> next day we learned that the Nazis had run out of gas
> and the children had been hurled into the furnaces alive.

Debost asked Vaillant-Couturier how many of the 230 French-
women in her group survived Auschwitz. Forty-nine, she answered.

On her way out of the courtroom, she passed the prisoners'
dock and paused momentarily within a few feet of Göring. Later,
she wrote:

> I wanted to see them up close. I wanted to see the
> expressions on their faces. I looked at each of them in
> turn. They looked like ordinary people with a normal,
> human side, which somehow didn't surprise me. At
> Auschwitz, one of the SS used to bring sugar to a five-
> year-old gypsy boy after he gassed the boy's mother and
> sister.

The testimony of Vaillant-Couturier and others about the horrors of the concentration camps proved to be the most damning
evidence of all to those defendants in any way associated with the
camps. The "ordinary people" most heavily implicated by the
French prosecution's evidence were Speer, Göring, Seyss-Inquart,
Sauckel, Rosenberg, Keitel, and Jodl.

After a forceful, often heartrending presentation, the French
advocates concluded their case on February 7. The Soviets
began theirs the next day.

The Soviet Case

On the morning of February 8, spectators thronged excitedly
into Room 600 of Nuremberg's Palace of Justice in anticipation
of hearing from the Soviets for the first time. They wondered
what, if anything, the Soviets would say about the Nazi-Soviet
nonaggression pact of 1939, in which the two parties agreed to
divide and occupy Poland; or about the Soviet attack on Finland
in 1940. (Although both issues proved embarrassing to the Soviets, neither issue impacted the trial in any substantive manner.)

Captain Gilbert remarked to Göring "that the courtroom was full for the first time in weeks." Gilbert recalled that Göring, who had persistently called the trial a mockery of justice, looked depressed. The chief Nazi defendant replied gloomily, "Yes, they want to see the show. You will see—this trial will be a disgrace in 15 years." His opinion had not changed.

Soviet chief prosecutor Lieutenant General Roman A. Rudenko stepped up to the lectern and launched an oral assault on the "Hitlerites" and "fascist aggressors" who had attacked the "peace-loving" countries of Europe. Rudenko, bearish of figure, and lacking the oratory polish of his predecessors, made up for his shortcomings of form and style by stating plain truths simply. He told the tribunal that it was time to punish "those who organized and were guilty of monstrous crimes." Rudenko said in conclusion:

> In the name of the sacred memory of millions of innocent victims of the fascist terror, for the sake of the consolidation of peace throughout the world, for the sake of the future security of nations, we are presenting the defendants a just and complete bill which must be paid. This is a bill on behalf of all mankind, a bill backed by the will and the consciences of all freedom-loving nations. May justice be done.

Upon completing his opening address, Rudenko yielded the podium to his deputy chief prosecutor, Colonel Yuri V. Pokrovsky, who began presenting the Soviet evidence.

Surprise Witness

One of the highlights of the Soviet presentation came on February 11. Rudenko surprised everyone in the courtroom by calling Field Marshal Friedrich Paulus to the witness box. No one (except the Soviets) had known of Paulus's availability as a witness, and thus no one had anticipated his appearance in court.

Paulus had commanded the German Sixth Army during the siege of Stalingrad. His live testimony added a fascinating dimension to the trials, exciting the court and further incriminating several of the defendants.

Friedrich Paulus, called by the Soviet prosecuting team, gives evidence against his fellow military leaders during the Nuremberg trials.

Rudenko: Who of the defendants was an active participant in the initiation of a war of aggression against the Soviet Union?

Paulus: Of the defendants . . . the Chief of the Supreme Command of the Armed Forces, Keitel; Chief of the Operations Branch, Jodl; and Göring, in his capacity as Reich Marshal, as Commander-in-Chief of the Air Forces, and as Plenipotentiary [agent with full power to transact business] for Armament Economy.

Rudenko: . . . Have I rightly concluded from your testimony, that long before 22 June [the date of the German invasion] the Hitlerite Government and the Supreme Command of the Armed Forces were planning an aggressive war against the Soviet Union for the purpose of colonizing the territory of the Soviet Union?

Paulus: That is beyond doubt according to all the developments as I described them and also in connection with all the directives issued.

Rudenko asked no further questions, and the defense counsel for the general staff deferred cross-examination until the following morning. Several German defense counselors cross-examined Paulus the next day. Paulus, though nervous, held firm in his surprise testimony.

Making Soap

As the Soviet case evolved, entries presented from Hans Frank's diary clearly showed his involvement with Nazi atrocities in Poland's death camps. A Soviet film entitled *The Atrocities by the German Fascist Invaders in the U.S.S.R.* numbed the senses of those who viewed it. Captain Gilbert described it as "even more terrible than the one presented by the Americans." While images of obscenities flashed upon the screen, Göring pretended to read a book and occasionally yawned in feigned boredom.

For four days the Soviets assaulted the sensibility of the court with a barrage of depositions and live-witness testimony describing how the Nazis exploited human beings. Perhaps none of the testimony was more grotesque or disturbing than the details of how the Nazis made soap from human corpses. John Henry Witton, a former British prisoner of war whom the Nazis had employed at the Danzig Anatomic Institute, recalled:

> The corpses arrived at an average of seven to eight per day. All of them had been beheaded and were naked. The corpses were unloaded as quickly as possible and taken down into the cellar. They were then put in large metal containers where they were then left for approximately four months. Owing to the preservative mixture in which they were stored, the tissue came away from the bones very easily. The tissue was then put in a boiler about the size of a kitchen table.

William Neely, another British prisoner of war, remembered:

> A machine for the manufacture of soap was completed sometime in March or April 1944. It consisted, as far as I remember, of an electrically heated tank in which bones of the corpses were mixed with some acid and melted down.

Sigmund Mazur, a German laboratory assistant at the institute, provided a recipe for soap:

> In February 1944 Professor Spanner [Mazur's superior] gave me the recipe for the preparation of soap from human fat. According to the recipe five kilos of human fat are mixed with ten liters of water and five hundred or one thousand grams of caustic soda. All this is boiled two or three hours and then cooled. The soap floats to the surface while the water and other sediment remain at the bottom. After having cooled, the soap is poured into molds. I boiled the soap out of the bodies of women and men. The process of boiling alone took several days— from three to seven. During two manufacturing processes, in which I directly participated, more than twenty-five kilograms [55 pounds] of soap were produced. The amount of human fat necessary for these two processes was seventy to eighty kilograms [154 to 176 pounds] collected from some forty bodies. The finished soap then went to Professor Spanner, who kept it personally. I used this soap for my personal needs, for toilet and for laundry.
>
> In the same way as for human fat, Professor Spanner ordered us to collect human skin, which after having been cleaned of fat was treated by certain chemical products. The finished skin was packed in boxes and used for special purposes which I don't know.

Assistant Soviet prosecutor L. N. Smirnov raised a few courtroom eyebrows when he offered a bar of soap and a piece of skin as evidence, followed by a presentation of slide projections. The slides showed photographs of baskets filled with guillotined heads found in Danzig, and snapshots of mass executions, the hanging of women, and streets lined with dead bodies. Göring grinned broadly when the first slide was inadvertently projected upside down.

Tales of Horror

Smirnov continued to hammer away at inhumane acts committed by the Nazis, honing in on the Nazi reign of terror against the

Slavic people. The Slavs who could not be used as slave laborers, he told the tribunal, were put to death in horrifying fashion. Nazi officials and their underlings needed indoctrination and training to carry out their murderous assignments. In Smirnov's words:

> In order to murder millions of innocent and defenseless people, it was necessary not only to develop the technical formula of "Cyclone A" [poison gas], to construct gas chambers and crematory ovens, nor only to elaborate a procedure for mass shootings. It was also essential to educate many thousands who would carry out these policies "not in the letter but in the spirit"—as stated by Himmler in one of his speeches. It was necessary to train persons deprived both of heart and conscience, perverted creatures who had deliberately cut themselves off from the basic concepts of morality and law.

Smirnov supported his theme with more eyewitness testimony. One ex-prisoner of the Nazis who had been assigned to burning bodies testified:

Containers of the poison gas Cyclone used to mass murder the Jews.

Yanov Camp was surrounded by a barbed wire entangle-
ment. . . . A man would be thrown in and left there for
several days on end. He could not extricate himself from
the wire and he eventually perished. . . . A man would be
strung up by the neck, hands, and feet. Dogs would be
set upon him and would tear him to pieces. Human
beings would be used as targets for shooting practice. . . . Men would be taken by the legs and torn in two.
Infants from 1 month to 3 years old were thrown in buck-
ets of water and left to drown. . . . Women were strung
up by the hair, after having been stripped naked, and left
to hang until they died.

Tales of unimaginable horror and uncountable slayings continued to stun a disbelieving courtroom assemblage for four
more days.

The Prosecution Rests

As the Soviet case neared its conclusion, Smirnov called
Auschwitz survivor Severina Schmaglevskaya to the stand. Captain Gilbert observed that "several defense attorneys bit their
lips" and "most of the defendants lowered their heads" as she
described "how Jewish children were thrown alive into crematorium furnaces during the rush season of 1944." Schmaglevskaya
concluded her testimony with a painfully touching question.
With repressed bitterness, she demanded, "In the name of all
the women of Europe who became mothers in concentration
camps, I would like to ask German mothers, 'Where are our children now?'"

Afterward, Dönitz's attorney asked him, "Didn't *anybody*
know *anything* about *any* of these things?" The old admiral could
only shake his head and shrug sadly. But *somebody* had to know
about "these things," or they would not have happened. Jodl
stated the obvious. "Of course somebody knew about it," he said
softly.

On March 4, 1946, the Soviets finished their case, and the
prosecution rested.

Chapter 5

The German Defense: Top Nazis and Capital Criminals

THE GERMAN DEFENSE BEGAN ITS ARGUMENTS on March 8, 1946. With only a handful of counselors and an inadequate backup staff, the German defenders operated at a disadvantage from the start. But the size of their staff was not their only handicap.

Under the terms of the IMT Charter, they could not question the legitimacy of the tribunal or its proceedings. Neither could they claim victors' justice nor offer a *tu quoque* ("so did you") argument by mentioning the deliberate Allied bombing of civilians during raids on several German cities.

Also, despite having to defend against charges of waging an aggressive war, the defense counselors were forbidden to call attention to the fact that two Soviet judges—representing a nation guilty of the same offense—sat on the bench. [The Soviets had waged an aggressive (undeclared) war against Finland in 1939 and against Japan in 1945.]

Allied prosecutors had relied on documentary evidence and eyewitness testimony to prove their case. By then, in the minds of most defense counselors and prosecutors alike, the prosecution had proved the fundamental criminality of the Nazi regime.

As to the individual defendants, the prosecutors had opted to present their evidence against them as part of their case against the Nazi regime, simply referring to those sections of the overall case for which each defendant bore responsibility. Hence, the defense task became one of disassociating individuals from the regime to prove their innocence—or to lessen their guilt.

In order to do so, the defense would have to show that the defendants had not taken part in the alleged "common plan" and had not been involved in violations of international laws or in crimes against humanity. The impression made by each defendant on the stand would therefore become critical to his defense. Each defendant took the stand in order of his indictment, beginning with the two top Nazis, Hermann Göring and Rudolf Hess.

The Top Nazi

The long-awaited moment when Reichsmarschall and second-leading Nazi Hermann Göring took the stand finally came on the afternoon of March 13. He appeared in court wearing a neatly pressed but ill-fitting dove gray uniform. The once corpulent German had lost seventy-six pounds in captivity on a diet imposed on him by the prison commandant. A wine-red scarf around his neck, reminiscent of his flying days, hid the signs of substantial weight loss. With trousers bloused over the top of his highly polished yellow boots, he strode purposefully to the witness box. He seemed determined to show the court, the German people, and the world at large that this man Göring was a soldier.

Under defense counsel Dr. Stahmer's questioning, Göring testified in his own behalf for two and a half days. Stahmer would ask short questions, and Göring, unrestricted by the tribunal, would give long answers. Prosecutor Jackson objected vigorously to Göring's lengthy responses, claiming them to be little more than Nazi propaganda, but Chief Justice Lawrence overruled his objections.

Stahmer asked Göring if he believed that the Nazi Party had assumed power legally. Göring replied with candor. "Once we came to power," he said, "we were determined to hold on to it under all circumstances. . . . We did not want to leave this any longer to chance, to elections and parliamentary majorities."

Unlike his codefendants, most of whom tried to minimize their responsibilities, Göring crowed to the court and cameras like a barnyard cock, seemingly eager to leave no doubt in anyone's mind as to the breadth of his influence and the importance of his role in the Nazi hierarchy.

> With the dynamic personality of the Führer, unsolicited advice was not in order, and one had to be on very good terms with him. That is to say, one had to have great influence, as I had.

"What about concentration camps?" Stahmer asked. Göring explained that they could not allow deadly enemies, particularly communists, to run free. Concentration camps were necessary to maintain order in the new regime. "It was a question of removing danger. Only one course was available, protective custody." Göring pointed out that the term "concentration camp" originated with the foreign press and not with the Nazis.

A Hallowed Image

Responding to the tribunal's charge that a conspiracy had existed, Göring dismissed it as simply ridiculous:

> One can only talk of conspiracy here to the extent that this took place between the Führer and me until, say, 1941. There was no one who could even approach working as closely with the Führer, who was essentially familiar with his thoughts, and who had the same influence as I. Therefore at best only the Führer and I could have conspired [and no one else].

Göring's codefendants welcomed their superior's unflinching willingness to accept responsibility. They hoped, of course, that Göring's testimony would dilute the question of their own guilt and enhance their chances for acquittal—or at least for survival. When Stahmer asked, "To what extent did you participate in issuing the Nuremberg Laws of 1935?" Göring replied without hesitation:

Hermann Göring smiles while on the witness stand during the Nuremberg trials.

In my capacity as president of the Reichstag, I promulgated those laws here in Nuremberg, where the Reichstag was meeting at that time.

Göring's well-conceived answers suggested a man clearly dedicated to establishing a hallowed personal image in history's hall of fame.

Words and Music

On the third and last day of his testimony, Göring refuted charges brought against the Luftwaffe for bombing Rotterdam *after* the Netherlands had surrendered. He said that orders to call off the bombing attack had come too late. Rather than an atrocity, Göring argued, Rotterdam had been a tragic mistake.

Stahmer, in a last question, asked Göring about Germany's behavior with regard to the rules of civilized conduct. The Nazi chief replied that the dynamics of modern warfare had eclipsed the policies established at the Hague and Geneva Conventions.

> At this point, I should like to say the very words which one of our greatest, most important and strongest opponents, the British prime minister Winston Churchill, used: "In the struggle for life and death, there is, in the end, no legality."

Churchill had actually said: "There could be no justice, if in a mortal struggle, the aggressor tramples down every sentiment of humanity, and if those who resist remain entangled in the tatters of violated legal conventions." Göring changed the lyrics, but the melody remained uncomfortably the same.

"Saved by the Bell"

On March 18 at 12:10 P.M., the pudgy, bulldoglike Jackson strode to the prosecution stand with jutted chin and pugnacious self-assurance. To the surprise of the crowded courtroom, Jackson opened his cross-examination in a mild manner, asking Göring, "You are perhaps aware that you are the only man living who can expound to us the true purpose of the Nazi Party and the inner workings of its leadership?" Spectators stirred and buzzed in amazement.

"I am perfectly aware of that," Göring answered.

Jackson later disclosed that he had decided on a strategy of first flattering the Nazi chief and then hitting him hard. But his hard blows either fell short or went wide of the mark. Ten minutes into his interrogation of Göring, it became clear that Jackson was in trouble.

U.S. prosecutor Robert H. Jackson led the American team's questioning of the Nazis. Göring outsmarted Jackson on several occasions during Jackson's examination of him.

When Jackson asked if it were not true that the Nazis had meant to overthrow the Weimar government, Göring unblinkingly replied, "That was my firm intention." And was it not true that on assuming power the Nazis had eliminated democratic government? "We found it no longer necessary," said the foxy Göring.

Jackson continued with a series of questions about the concentration camps. When Göring began another of his lengthy answers, Jackson interrupted him and demanded a yes-or-no answer to his questions. Göring insisted that he needed to explain. Jackson advised him that explanations could be explored during redirect examination by his own counsel.

At that point Chief Justice Lawrence intervened in Göring's behalf. "Mr. Jackson," Sir Geoffrey said, "the tribunal thinks the witness ought to be allowed to make what explanation he thinks right in answer to the question." Sir Geoffrey intended to ensure that there would be no future charges of unfair bias in his court. Jackson seethed in silent disgust.

In his anger Jackson seemed to lose control of his voluminous material. On one occasion he asked, "And who was your Reich Commissar in Poland?"

Göring was obviously enjoying the mismatch. "There was no Reich Commissar in Poland," he said. "There was a governor-general in Poland, and he was Dr. Frank."

In another instance Jackson quoted from a document intended to show that the Nazis had violated the Treaty of Versailles by plotting "the liberation of the Rhineland." Göring, with a copy of the same report, explained that Jackson had mistranslated it. The document referred to the Rhine River, not the Rhineland. And it spoke of "clearing" the river of navigational hazards, not of "liberation." The smug Göring was correct. Jackson, perhaps driven by the bulldog in him, refused to let go.

"Were not these actions part of a plan to rearm the Rhineland?" he asked. And were not these plans "kept entirely secret from foreign powers?" Göring again made Jackson pay.

"I do not think I can recall reading beforehand the publication of the mobilization preparations of the United States," he snarled.

At the end of the session, a journalist in the balcony was heard to say of Jackson, "Saved by the bell."

Redemption

Jackson finally started to penetrate Göring's defenses the next day, moving the questioning to *Kristallnacht* (Night of Broken Glass). On the night of November 9, 1938, following the murder of a Nazi official (allegedly) by a seventeen-year-old Jewish refugee boy, Nazi storm troopers and ruffians had looted and destroyed 815 Jewish shops and 76 synagogues all across Germany. Twenty thousand Jews had been arrested, of whom thirty-six died.

Göring later summoned Joseph Goebbels, Walther Funk, Reinhard Heydrich—then members of Göring's air ministry—and an insurance adjuster to discuss damage claims. Jackson now read a documented word-for-word exchange between Göring and the adjuster, who had pointed out that many of the claims came from non-Jewish owners of goods consigned to the devastated Jewish shops.

Hermann Göring claps his hand over his mouth after uttering a remark out of turn at the Nuremberg trials.

Of this, Göring had said to Heydrich, "I wish you had killed two hundred Jews instead of destroying such valuables." Göring next informed the adjuster that he intended to save the insurance industry millions by denying all Jewish claims. He then told the insurance representative, "All of a sudden an angel, in my somewhat corpulent shape, appears before you. I should like to go fifty-fifty with you." Göring grudgingly admitted the quotations.

Jackson kept up the pressure. He read Göring's verbatim remarks from the close of that meeting eight years earlier:

> I demand that German Jewry shall for their abominable crimes make a contribution of a million marks. That will work. The pigs will not commit a second murder so quickly. I would not like to be a Jew in Germany.

Jackson asked Göring if the statement was accurate. A dejected Göring said it was. Having partially redeemed himself, Jackson then turned over the lectern to British prosecutor Maxwell-Fyfe.

Göring Stumbles

Göring's guilt on all counts had already been established beyond any question under the weight of evidence presented earlier. Sir David Maxwell-Fyfe added an exclamation point.

Roaring to the attack, Sir David took direct aim at Göring's complicity in the slaughter of fifty captured British flyers who had escaped from Stalag Luft III (a prison camp). Göring had denied any knowledge of their murders, claiming to have been on leave at the time. Sir David scoffed at Göring's denial:

> **Maxwell-Fyfe:** I am suggesting to you that it is absolutely impossible that, in these circumstances, you knew absolutely nothing about it.

> **Göring:** Field Marshal Milch was here as a witness, and, regrettably, was not asked about these points.

> **Maxwell-Fyfe:** Oh, yes he was. . . . Both you and Milch are now trying to shift the responsibility onto the shoulders of your junior officers.

Göring: [Upset by the attack on his honor] That's untrue.

Maxwell-Fyfe: You did nothing to prevent these men from being shot. You cooperated in this foul series of murders.

Göring: I did not hear about this incident until after it occurred [insisting that he had been on leave at the time].

Sir David then read from the Nazi chief's personnel file. Göring had indeed been on leave until March 29, 1944. But the slaughter of the fifty British airmen had gone on until April 13. Sir David had dug a hole and Göring had stumbled into it.

A Quiet Ending

With Göring in the hole, Sir David shoveled dirt in after him, next attacking the number-two Nazi's unstinting devotion to Adolf Hitler. "Now, I want to be perfectly fair," Sir David began, then boldly accused Göring of murder.

Maxwell-Fyfe: Let me remind you of the affidavit of Hoettl of the RSHA [Reich Central Security Office]. He says that approximately four million Jews have been killed in the concentration camps, while an additional two million met death in other ways. . . . Are you telling this tribunal that a minister with your power in the Reich could remain ignorant that this was going on?

Göring: These things were kept secret from me. I might add that, in my opinion, not even the Führer knew the extent of what was going on.

Sir David then read from a report containing Hitler's comments to Hungarian leader Miklós Horthy: "The Jews have been treated as germs with which a healthy body has been infected. There are only a few Jews left alive. Tens of thousands have been disposed of."

THE FOX AND THE BEAR

On cross-examination, Roman Rudenko, the chief Soviet prosecutor, asked Hermann Göring about how much of the Soviet Union Germany had ultimately intended to annex. The inquiry produced a typical exchange between the bearlike Rudenko and the foxy Göring.

Göring: Had we been victorious . . . after the signing of the peace we would . . . have decided how far the annexation would serve our purposes. . . .

Rudenko: I understand you . . . after the war was won you would have seized these provinces [Soviet territory up to the Ural Mountains] and annexed them. In principle you have not protested.

Göring: Not in principle. As an old hunter, I acted according to the principle of not dividing the bear's skin before the bear was shot. . . .

Rudenko: Luckily, this did not happen.

Göring: Luckily for you.

In this exchange, the fox appeared to have separated the bear from his skin. Shortly after this encounter, however, Rudenko elicited an admission from Göring that his responsibilities extended to the forced-labor programs. This admission was sufficient to prove his guilt on charges based on counts three and four of the indictment (war crimes and crimes against humanity).

Maxwell-Fyfe: Do you say neither Hitler nor you knew of the policy to exterminate Jews?

Göring: As far as Hitler is concerned, I have said I do not think so. As far as I am concerned, I have said that I did not know, even approximately, to what extent these things were taking place.

Maxwell-Fyfe: You did not know to what degree, but you knew there was a policy that aimed at the extermination of the Jews?

Göring: No, a policy of emigration, not liquidation of the Jews. I knew only that there had been isolated cases of such perpetrations.

On that hollow note, Sir David yielded to Soviet prosecutor Roman Rudenko, who grilled Göring in anticlimactic fashion about German annexations in eastern Europe.

On March 22 French prosecutor Champetier de Ribes declined to cross-examine Göring, and Göring's defense ended quietly.

Hess's Higher Tribunal

The most serious charges against Rudolf Hess, the one-time third-ranking Nazi, was that he had slavishly followed Hitler's bidding and had dutifully supported the repressive measures inflicted on the Jews and Poles. His flight to Scotland in 1941 precluded his participation in subsequent Nazi atrocities. Shortly before his case was to be heard, the question on everyone's lips was, "Will Hess take the stand in his own behalf?" Dr. Alfred Seidl, Hess's defense counsel, kept the court waiting for the answer.

Accused Nazi Rudolf Hess never testified in his own defense at Nuremberg.

Seidl first called on two defense witnesses who testified weakly, then he offered an equally weak diversionary defense based on the "unjust" (to the Germans) provisions of the Treaty of Versailles. The tribunal flatly dismissed his argument. However unjust the defense might find the treaty, the tribunal ruled, no injustice contained in it could possibly justify the war started by the Nazis, or the war's ensuing horrors.

At that point Seidl surprised everyone by revealing that Hess would not take the stand. The defense rested. Seidl had not provided Hess with much of a defense. Nor had Hess done much to help himself. Hess later complained to Göring, "I know now that the Nuremberg proceedings will never end—we will have to answer to a higher tribunal." Rudolf Hess had apparently already committed his fate "to a higher tribunal."

The Malevolent Seven

The evidence against the next seven defendants—Ribbentrop, Keitel, Kaltenbrunner, Rosenberg, Frank, Frick, and Streicher—was particularly damning and left little doubt as to their conviction. Ribbentrop took the stand on April 1.

Ribbentrop protested his innocence of all involvement in Nazi aggressions, but prosecutors shredded his claims of purity on cross-examination. When grilled about his part in seizing foreign territories and in persecuting Jews as a member of the SS, the wavering minister resorted to an "I know nothing" defense.

When the groveling foreign minister finished testifying, Göring, with undisguised contempt, said to Ribbentrop, "You were not even interesting."

In writing his final testament, Hitler had blamed Wilhelm Keitel, the ranking officer of the Wehrmacht, and the High Command for Germany's defeat. Keitel walked with soldierly bearing to the witness box, soon to be humbled by the prosecution. Following a passive defense, Keitel admitted on cross-examination that he had done much that was "against the inner voice of my conscience."

Britain's Maxwell-Fyfe asked him to name three such things. Staring straight ahead and speaking deliberately, Keitel complied:

> [First were] the orders given for the conduct of the war in the East, which were contrary to the accepted uses of warfare. The question [execution] of the fifty RAF fliers [at Stalag Luft III]. And, worst of all, the *Nacht und Nebel* [Night and Fog] decree. . . . I personally thought that to deport individuals secretly was much crueler than a death sentence. [The Night and Fog Decree was Hitler's

order to seize persons "endangering German security" in the West and make them disappear into the night and fog of the unknown in Germany.]

Maxwell-Fyfe asked no further questions. Upon Keitel's return to the dock, Göring snarled, "Why didn't you say anything about how the Allies treated our saboteurs? You bungled it!"

Among the prosecutors, Ernst Kaltenbrunner easily won honors as the most revolting Nazi on trial. When questioned about his signature on thousands of orders sending people to their deaths in concentration camps, he said, "Not once in my whole life did I ever see or sign a single protective custody order." The prosecutors could not stifle their laughter. Even Kaltenbrunner's defense counsel, Kurt Kauffmann, commented that "this statement of yours is not very credible. It is a monstrosity." Few disagreed.

General Wilhelm Keitel (standing) pleads not guilty to his indictment. Keitel later admitted that he had acted against his conscience during the war.

Alfred Rosenberg, the former Nazi minister for the Occupied Eastern Territories, had planned the rape of Russia, comfortable in the knowledge that his actions would result in the deaths of millions. He later objected to some of the killings of slave laborers, but he lacked the moral courage to protest to Hitler.

"I did not see Hitler as a tyrant," Rosenberg told the tribunal, "but like many millions of National Socialists I trusted him personally on the strength of the experience of a fourteen-year-long struggle."

Hans Frank entered the witness box on April 18. The ex-governor-general of Poland testified with remorse. He told the court, "A thousand years will pass and still Germany's guilt will not have been erased." It appeared that Frank intended to go to the gallows, if fate so willed it, with a clear conscience.

Wilhelm Frick, the former Nazi minister of defense and strong enforcer of the Nuremberg Laws, opted not to testify.

Julius Streicher, notorious "Jew-baiter" and purveyor of racial hate doctrines, served his own cause poorly on the stand. In *Der Stürmer*, his newspaper, he had referred to the Jews as "a nation of bloodsuckers and extortionists." Asked by a British prosecutor if that was not "preaching race hatred," the squat, bald Streicher replied, "No. It is not preaching hatred. It is a statement of fact." And so it went.

Chapter 6

The German Defense: Bankers, Admirals, and the Last Nine

G ÖRING'S CASE HAD TAKEN TWELVE COURT DAYS, largely because the tribunal had allowed the rotund Nazi to ramble almost at will. The remaining twenty defendants were not accorded equal time for rambling monologues, however, or the trial might have dragged on for a year or more. Hence, with the exception of Göring, individual trials averaged about four days each and lasted until the end of June. The cases yet to be heard were those of the bank presidents, the fleet admirals, and the remaining nine Nazis.

Two for the Money

In order of indictment, Walther Funk was scheduled to appear after Streicher. But since Hjalmar Schacht had preceded Funk as both minister of finance and president of the Reichsbank, Schacht took the stand first to facilitate a chronological presentation of the evidence. It was now April 30, 1946.

The sixty-nine-year-old Hjalmar Schacht owned the ablest mind among all the defendants. With an IQ of 143, Schacht was the only prisoner to testify in English, staunchly denying that he had helped plan and carry out aggressive warfare. After delaying a decision to take part in the assassination attempt on Hitler (July 1944), Schacht was imprisoned at Dachau and later liberated by American troops. His fall from grace could only help his defense.

Former president of the Reichsbank Hjalmar Schacht was imprisoned at Dachau by Hitler in 1944.

On cross-examination, Jackson tried to tie the silver-haired banker to Hitler's expansionist policy. He pointed out that Schacht had assimilated Sudetenland funds into the Reichsbank to assist in Germany's absorption of that country.

Jackson: That is what you did after this wrong and reprehensible act had been committed by Hitler, did you not?

Schacht: It is no "wrong and reprehensible" act committed by Hitler, but Hitler received the Sudeten German territory by way of treaty. There can be no talk of injustice. I cannot believe that the Allies have put their signature to a piece of injustice.

Jackson: The taking over of Czechoslovakia representing your idea of justice?

Schacht: I have already told you that Germany did not "take over Czechoslovakia," but that it was indeed presented to Germany by the Allies on a silver platter.

Jackson recounted the invasions of Poland, Luxembourg, and other nations. Schacht conceded that the invasions had been unqualified acts of aggression, adding that Jackson had "left out Norway and Belgium." The pugnacious prosecutor continued:

Jackson: Yes; well, I got to the end of my paper. The entire course was a course of aggression?

Schacht: Absolutely to be condemned.

Jackson: And the success of that aggression at every step was due to the Wehrmacht, which you had to do so much with creating?

Schacht: Unfortunately.

Although Jackson appeared to have scored a victory in eliciting a few concessions from Schacht, the tenor of the moment suggested that Schacht stood the best chance of any defendant for acquittal.

Banker Walther Funk stood indicted under counts one and two for promoting "the accession to power of the Nazi conspirators and the consolidation of their control over Germany." Funk had accepted unusual bank deposits consisting of valuables that had once been the property of Nazi death camp victims. Funk denied having known of the sources of the often grotesque deposits. Associate U.S. prosecutor Thomas Dodd attacked his denial:

Dodd: When did you start to do business with the SS, Mr. Funk?

Funk: Business with the SS? I have never done that.

Dodd: Yes, sir, business with the SS. . . . You were not ordinarily in the habit, in the Reichsbank, of accepting jewels, monocles, spectacles, watches, cigarette cases, pearls, diamonds, gold dentures, were you?

Funk: If that happened, then the Reichsbank committed an illegal act. The Reichsbank was not authorized to do that.

Dodd: And it is your statement that if it was done you did not know anything about it?

Funk: No [meaning yes].

Dodd then showed a brief movie picturing the contents of the Reichsbank vaults in Frankfurt. Huge, unsealed sacks spilled out

Banker Walther Funk denied knowledge of the deposits of jewelry and other valuables found in the Reichsbank after the war. These valuables were taken from murdered Jews.

a potpourri of bracelets, rings, watches, jewelry, gold coins, and gold teeth. Funk again denied any knowledge of the odd deposits, but the filmed evidence loomed large in the eyes of the tribunal.

Two from the Sea

The principal charge against Grand Admiral Karl Dönitz cited "crimes against persons and property at sea." A directive issued by Dönitz known as the Laconia Order figured prominently in his indictment. *Laconia* was a twenty-thousand-ton British liner torpedoed in the South Atlantic by a German U-boat. The order prohibited the rescue of survivors of ships sunk by U-boats. An affidavit from Admiral Chester Nimitz, commander of the U.S. Pacific Fleet, helped to ease the order's damaging effect on Dönitz's defense. The affidavit stated that American submarines had operated in a similar fashion against the Japanese in the Pacific.

> **Interrogator:** Was it customary for submarines to attack merchantmen without warning?

Nimitz: Yes, with the exception of hospital ships and other vessels under safe conduct voyages for humanitarian purposes.

Interrogator: Were, by order or on general principles, the U.S. submarines prohibited from carrying out rescue measures toward passengers and crews of ships sunk without warning in those cases where by doing so the safety of their own boat was endangered?

Nimitz: On general principles, the U.S. submarines did not rescue enemy survivors if undue additional hazard to the submarine resulted, or the submarine would be prevented from accomplishing its further mission. Therefore, it was unsafe to pick up many survivors.

The weight of the great American admiral's words may well have tipped the scales of military justice in the Nazi admiral's favor.

The case against Grand Admiral Erich Raeder, who preceded Dönitz as commander in chief of the German navy, mainly alleged that he had violated the Treaty of Versailles by building up the German navy. Soviet prosecutor Rudenko read a statement that Raeder had made while a Soviet prisoner in Moscow, unburdening himself of resentment toward Speer, Dönitz, Keitel, and Göring:

Speer flattered Dönitz's vanity and vice versa. Dönitz's strong political party inclinations brought him difficulties as head of the navy. His last speech to the Hitler Youth, which was ridiculed in all circles, gave him the nickname of *"Hitlerbube Dönitz"* ["Hitlerboy Dönitz"]. . . . [Keitel was] a man of unimaginable weakness, who owes his long stay in his position to this characteristic. The Führer could treat him as badly as he wished—he stood for it. . . . Göring had a disastrous effect on the fate of the German Reich. His main peculiarities were unimaginable vanity and immeasurable ambition, running after popularity and showing off, untruthfulness, impracticality, and selfishness. He was outstanding in his greed, wastefulness, and soft unsoldierly manner.

The seventy-year-old admiral's unflattering appraisals of his Nazi colleagues did little to help his defense, nor did they succeed in winning the hearts of his countrymen. A seething Dönitz called him "a pissed-off jealous old man!"

At that point in his life, Raeder showed little concern. He later told Captain Gilbert, "Naturally, I will be hanged or shot. I flatter myself to think I will be shot. I have no desire to serve a prison sentence at my age." Raeder's desire would not influence the tribunal.

Nine for the Crime

Baldur von Schirach took the stand on May 23. Sauckel, Jodl, Bormann (in absentia), Papen, Seyss-Inquart, Speer, Neurath, and Fritzsche followed him into the witness box.

Baldur von Schirach, ex-head of the Hitler Youth, once said to his American cell guard, "Our Hitler Youth was the same as your Boy Scouts." In court, he admitted knowing about the mass exterminations in the east. And he confessed, "I alone bear the guilt for having trained our young people . . . for a man [Hitler]

While testifying in his defense, Baldur von Schirach, head of the Hitler Youth, called Hitler a murderer.

A Murderous Principle

The stone-faced, never-smiling General Alfred Jodl defended to the very end his leadership and the actions of the Wehrmacht. He contended that his role in preparing the plans for all of Hitler's aggressions had been purely strategic and nonpolitical.

On cross-examination, British assistant prosecutor Geoffrey Roberts questioned Jodl about Hitler's Partisan Order, which specified that resistance should not be punished "by legal prosecution of the guilty, but by the occupation forces spreading such terror as is alone appropriate to eradicate every inclination to resist." Roberts matched Jodl's cynicism with sarcasm.

Roberts: That is a terrible order, is it not?

Jodl: No, it is not at all terrible, for it is established by international law that the inhabitants of an occupied territory must follow the orders and instructions of the occupying power, and any uprising, any resistance against the army occupying the country is forbidden. . . .

Roberts: I will not argue about it, witness. I gather you approve of the order.

Jodl: I approve of it as a justified measure conforming to international law and directed against a widespread resistance movement which employed unscrupulous methods.

Jodl pointed out that, despite his support of the Partisan Order, he had subsequently issued an order on May 6, 1944, directing that in the future "all partisans captured in enemy uniform or civilian clothing or surrendering during combat are to be treated in principle as prisoners of war."

Jodl: [I took] this unusual step because I became convinced, after the shooting of the English Air Force officers [from Stalag Luft III] at Sagan, that the Führer no longer concerned himself with the idea of human rights. [In truth, Jodl issued the order because it had become necessary to utilize all available manpower for war production.]

Roberts: Had you thought that he was humane up to March of 1944?

Jodl: Before this time, I personally knew of no action of his which could not be justified legally, at least under international law.

Roberts: This was—would you agree with me—that this was sheer murder of these fifty airmen?

Jodl: I completely agree with you; I consider it sheer murder.

who murdered by the millions." The judges seemed to be receptive to Schirach's repentance. Psychologist Gilbert, who had counseled him to confess, was pleased.

Fritz Sauckel, bald-headed and wearing a Hitler-like mustache, tried to shift the blame for importing and mistreating more than five million workers. He told the tribunal, "My office had to meet the demands made by Speer." He defended his actions as head of the German conscript labor movement with a tirade of Low German grammar and worn Nazi phrases.

General Alfred Jodl's defense attempted to show him as a major influence in tempering Hitler's worst impulses. In his own behalf, the former operations chief of the German armed forces testified that he was among the few officers "who dared look the Führer squarely in the face and speak in a tone and manner that made listeners hold their breath because they feared catastrophe." But the prosecution revealed the German militarist side of Jodl that was willing to accept orders dutifully with blind obedience.

Martin Bormann's lawyer, Friedrich Bergold, made short work of Bormann's trial in absentia by declaring his client dead. Human remains, identified as Bormann's, were discovered in Berlin in 1972.

"A Civilized and Sympathetic Character"

On June 20 the last major defendant took the stand in the person of Albert Speer (who actually followed Papen in order of indictment and both Seyss-Inquart and Papen in order of trial). A brilliant, polished figure, the former Reich minister for armament and war production chastised Hitler with courageous composure. And he accepted responsibility for his own actions, stating:

> I, as an important member of the leadership of the Reich, share in the total responsibility. Hitler intended, deliberately, to destroy the means of life for his own people if the war were lost. I have no intention of using my actions [which had impeded Hitler's plans] during that phase of the war to help me in my personal defense.

And he did not. Speer's forthrightness earned the respect of U.S. chief prosecutor Jackson. The dark-eyed armaments chief, balding but still ruggedly handsome, went on to renounce the oath of loyalty to Hitler, which many of his predecessors had heavily relied upon in their defense.

> There is one loyalty which everyone must keep; and that is loyalty to one's own people. That duty comes before everything. If I am in a leading position and if I see that the interests of a nation are acted against in such a way, then I too must act. That Hitler had broken faith with the nation must have been clear to every intelligent member of his entourage, certainly at the latest in January or February 1945. Hitler had once been given his mission by the people; he had no right to gamble away the destiny of his people with his own.

As for the führer concept (which gave Hitler total control over Germans and their destiny), Speer said:

> Even in an authoritarian system the leaders must accept a common responsibility, and it is impossible for them to dodge that common responsibility after the catastrophe, for if the war had been won the leaders would also presumably have laid claim to common responsibility.

Speer's forthright acceptance of personal responsibility made him unique among his peers. As British prosecutor Maxwell-Fyfe wrote later, "Speer's consciousness of, and deep shame for, his own and Germany's crimes were in marked contrast with the rest of the defendants, and made him a civilized and sympathetic character."

The German Defense Ends

The defenses of the final four defendants—Papen, Seyss-Inquart, Neurath, and Fritzsche—were unexceptional and insignificant in the overall context of the trial.

Artur Seyss-Inquart (who preceded Papen to the stand at his request) testified truthfully with fatalistic resignation. "Whatever I say, my rope is being woven with Dutch hemp," he conceded, with a caustic reference to his role as commissioner of occupied Holland.

Franz von Papen, the diplomat, asserted that he "was not anti-Semitic," and that he was a patriot who had followed the Nazi doctrine out of love for his country. "I did my duty," he said.

The seventy-three-year-old Konstantin von Neurath, the ex-Protector of Bohemia and Moravia, suffered from near-senility. He rambled aimlessly for hours on the stand, until, to the relief of a handful of reporters present, his defense ended.

Hans Fritzsche, who had headed radio operations in the Nazi propaganda ministry, denied having known of the Final Solution. A smooth talker, he knew exactly what to say to impress the tribunal. Denouncing the Nazi dogma, Fritzsche said, "An ideology in the name of which five million people were murdered is a theory which cannot continue to exist." Fritzsche left the witness box on June 28, and the German defense ended.

Chapter 7

Judgment at Nuremberg

T HE DEFENSE SUMMATIONS BEGAN on July 4, 1946, and lasted for sixteen trial days. Prosecution summations required an additional three days. July slipped away but the trial continued for another month while the indicted Nazi organizations blamed one another for war crimes and atrocities.

No Laughing Matter

On August 31, 1946, the defendants made their last speeches, and the trial ended. In his final speech, in what was perhaps a too little and too late attempt to survive Nuremberg, Göring repudiated Hitler and proclaimed his own innocence. He appealed to God and the German people as witnesses to his claim of having acted purely out of patriotism.

The aged Franz von Papen, infuriated by Göring's hypocrisy, challenged him at lunch. "Who in the world is responsible for all this destruction if not you! You were the second man in the State! Is *nobody* responsible for any of this?" The old man waved his arm toward the rubble heaps of Nuremberg visible through the lunchroom window. Göring folded his arms defiantly and smirked at the old diplomat.

"Well, why don't you take the responsibility then?" Göring replied. "You were the Vice-Chancellor!"

Papen's face reddened. "I am taking my share of the responsibility!" he snapped. "But what about you? You haven't taken

As their sentences are read, the faces of the convicted Nazis reveal several different emotions.

the least responsibility for anything! All you do is make bombastic speeches! It is disgraceful!" Göring laughed. But it was no laughing matter.

The Verdicts

On September 30 and October 1, 1946, the tribunal at last rendered its verdicts, and its judgment on each of the twenty-one defendants was read: Schacht, Papen, and Fritzsche were found not guilty. The rest were adjudged guilty of one or more counts of the four-count indictment.

Prison psychologist G. M. Gilbert greeted each defendant as he returned from sentencing to the cellblock. Göring came down first, his face stiff and pale, his eyes bulging. "Death!" he said. He dropped to his cot and reached for a book with trembling hands, struggling to keep his composure. He asked to be left alone for a little while. The parade of condemned men continued.

Next came Hess: life in prison. Then Ribbentrop and Keitel: death by hanging. And Kaltenbrunner, Rosenberg, Frank, Frick, and Streicher: all death by hanging. Dönitz, ten years; and

Raeder, life. Sauckel and Jodl followed: death by hanging. Bormann, in absentia, was sentenced to hang. Speer and Neurath drew prison terms of twenty and fifteen years, respectively.

Among the seven Nazi organizations indicted, the tribunal delivered a criminal judgment against the Nazi Party Leadership, the SS, the Gestapo, and the SD. The SA, the Reich cabinet, and the High Command were acquitted of guilt. Members of the first four organizations were thus guilty of crimes by association. The tribunal adjudged that the SA (Brownshirts) and the Reich cabinet had lost their significance in the early 1930s. And the High Command involved so few officers, in the tribunal's judgment, that individual trials were preferable to a blanket ruling.

Last Words

Reich Marshal Hermann Göring cheated the hangman on the evening of October 15, 1946, with the bitter almond taste of cyanide on his lips. It was believed but never proved that an American officer whom he had befriended smuggled the lethal capsule to him. Göring left a parting note for his captors:

Hermann Göring (left) and Rudolf Hess listen to the verdict of the war crimes tribunal with dismay and dejection.

Seven of the defendants at Nuremberg listen to the reading of the verdict.
Hans Frank, Wilhelm Frick, and Julius Streicher (front, left to right) are
sentenced to hang.

To the Allied Control Council:

I would have had no objection to being shot. However, I
will not facilitate execution of Germany's *Reichsmarschall*
by hanging! For the sake of Germany, I cannot permit
this. Moreover, I feel no moral obligation to submit to
my enemies' punishment. For this reason, I have chosen
to die like the great Hannibal.

He signed the note with a sweeping hand. Then, in a last letter
to his wife, Emmy, his tone softened:

My one and only sweetheart, after serious consideration
and sincere prayer to the Lord, I have decided to take my
own life, lest I be executed in so terrible a fashion by my
enemies. . . . My life came to an end when I bade you
farewell for the last time. . . . All my thoughts are with you
and Edda [his eight-year-old daughter] and my dearest
ones. My last heartbeats are for our great and eternal love.

At 11:40 P.M., Göring's guard discovered him as he lay dying. A few minutes later, the number-two Nazi was pronounced dead. The executions of his condemned colleagues commenced less than one and a half hours later.

On October 16 at 1:11 A.M., four guards and several officers led Joachim von Ribbentrop across the prison exercise yard to the gymnasium and the three recently constructed gallows within. Upon the request of an army colonel, the prisoner stated his name with a steady voice, then mounted the scaffold. When asked for his final words, Ribbentrop said, "My last wish is that Germany realize its destiny and that an understanding be reached between East and West. I wish peace to the world."

Master Sergeant John Woods, one of three American hangmen, dropped a noose around Ribbentrop's neck and then covered his head with a black hood. At 1:14 A.M. Woods pulled the lever to the gallows trapdoor and it sprang open. The first Nazi to be hanged disappeared through the trap without a sound. He was pronounced dead at 1:29 A.M.

Two minutes later, Field Marshal Wilhelm Keitel mounted the wooden steps to the second gallows. He could see the rope in the gallows next to him still twisting and turning. Standing ramrod straight, he faced the witnesses and said, "More than two million soldiers went to their death for the fatherland. I now join my sons." When the noose and hood dropped over his head, he shouted, *Alles für Deutschland! Deutschland über Alles!* ["Everything for Germany! Germany over all!"]

Ernst Kaltenbrunner climbed the steps to the third gallows. In an unexpectedly steady voice, he said:

> I served the German people and my fatherland with willing heart. I did my duty according to its laws. I am sorry that in her trying hour she was not led only by soldiers. I regret that crimes were committed in which I had no part. Good luck Germany.

Alfred Rosenberg went to his death without speaking. Hans Frank, subdued and polite, faced the hangman and said, "I pray God to receive me mercifully." Wilhelm Frick stumbled on the

RESULTS OF THE NUREMBERG
IMT PROCEEDINGS

The following table offers a composite overview of the results of the trials of twenty-two major Nazi war criminals at Nuremberg.

Defendant*	Count 1	Count 2	Count 3	Count 4	Sentence
Hermann Göring	G	G	G	G	Hanging
Rudolf Hess	G	G	NG	NG	Life
Joachim von Ribbentrop	G	G	G	G	Hanging
Wilhelm Keitel	G	G	G	G	Hanging
Ernst Kaltenbrunner	NG	—	G	G	Hanging
Alfred Rosenberg	G	G	G	G	Hanging
Hans Frank	NG	—	G	G	Hanging
Wilhelm Frick	NG	G	G	G	Hanging
Julius Streicher	NG	—	—	G	Hanging
Walther Funk	NG	G	G	G	Life
Hjalmar Schacht	NG	NG	—	—	Acquitted
Karl Dönitz	NG	G	G	—	10 years
Erich Raeder	G	G	G	—	Life
Baldur von Schirach	NG	—	—	G	20 years
Fritz Sauckel	NG	NG	G	G	Hanging
Alfred Jodl	G	G	G	G	Hanging
Martin Bormann	NG	—	G	G	Hanging
Franz von Papen	NG	NG	—	—	Acquitted
Artur Seyss-Inquart	NG	G	G	G	Hanging
Albert Speer	NG	NG	G	G	20 years
Konstantin von Neurath	G	G	G	G	15 years
Hans Fritzsche	NG	—	NG	NG	Acquitted

*Listed in order of indictment. G=Guilty; NG=Not Guilty.

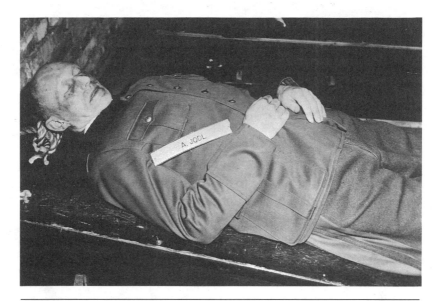

With the hangman's noose still around his neck, Alfred Jodl's body rests on a wooden coffin. Jodl was one of the top ten Nazis condemned to death at Nuremberg.

scaffold and said, "Let live the eternal Germany." Julius Streicher defiantly told Sergeant Woods, "Someday, the Bolsheviks will hang you!" When the hood was dropped over his head, Streicher said, "I am now by God my father. Adele my dear wife."

Fritz Sauckel angrily protested his innocence. "I die innocently. The verdict was wrong. God protect Germany and make Germany great again. Let Germany live and God protect my family." Alfred Jodl said only, "I salute you, my Germany."

Artur Seyss-Inquart, the last to die, departed with a selfless plea.

> I hope that this execution is the last act of the tragedy of the Second World War, and that a lesson will be learned so that peace and understanding will be realized among the nations. I believe in Germany.

He died at 2:57 A.M., less than two hours after Ribbentrop had climbed the gallows steps. Rightly or wrongly, the arch-Nazi war criminals had paid for their crimes.

Final Irony

The bodies of Göring and the ten hanged Nazis were placed face up in open wooden coffins and photographed by the U.S. Third Army photographer. Two trucks then transported the corpses through the early morning mist and rain to a crematorium near Munich. After cremation, the ashes were emptied into a small stream that flowed into the Isère River, then into the Danube, and ultimately into the Black Sea. It is interesting to think that, in some kind of final irony, a few of the ashes might have eventually washed ashore where Hitler's quest for *Lebensraum* had ended—on the sullied soil of the Soviet Union.

Afterword

The Nuremberg Legacy

AFTER RENDERING VERDICTS against the twenty-two major Nazi war criminals, the International Military Tribunal disbanded, its work completed. Chief U.S. prosecutor Robert Jackson submitted a final report to President Truman and returned to the bench of the U.S. Supreme Court. Telford Taylor, Jackson's assistant chief, took over the role of U.S. Chief Counsel for War Crimes. Taylor remained in Nuremberg for two and a half years to direct the U.S. prosecution of nearly two hundred lesser Nazi war criminals.

Twelve More Trials

The so-called second phase of the Nuremberg trials commenced in November 1946 and lasted until April 1949. U.S. military tribunals passed judgment on another 185 defendants. Responsibility for these trials fell entirely within the province of the United States. The variety and severity of the alleged offenses were such that international lawyers came to regard these trials as a most significant supplement to the earlier Nuremberg trial and to the Far East War Crimes trial in Tokyo. (An International Military Tribunal for the Far East [IMTFE] conducted war crimes trials against twenty-eight Japanese military and civilian leaders from May 1946 to November 1948. The IMTFE convicted all of the defendants, sentencing seven to be hanged and imprisoning the rest for terms ranging from seven years to life.)

The walled city of Nuremberg hosted one of the most famous trials in history.

The supplementary Nuremberg hearings were broken down into twelve trials. In connection with these trials, the U.S. military tribunals acquitted thirty-five defendants and released nineteen others on various grounds. Twenty-four of those charged were put to death, while twenty were sentenced to lifetime prison terms, and some eighty-seven others to shorter terms.

The Nuremberg Process

"The most significant thing about Nuremberg is that it happened," wrote assistant U.S. prosecutor Whitney R. Harris.

> More important than the punishment of the defendants, or the pronouncements of law, is the simple fact that for the first time in history the judicial process was brought to bear against those who had offended the conscience of humanity by committing acts of military aggression and other crimes.

SECOND-PHASE TRIALS

In recalling the Nuremberg trials, the prosecution of twenty-two major Nazi war criminals comes predominantly to the mind of most recallers. More often than not, the twelve subsequent trials held at Nuremberg between November 1946 and April 1949 generally escape recollection. These trials, conducted under the sole jurisdiction of U.S. military tribunals, are usually categorized as follows:

1. **The Medical Case:** Senior Nazi doctors charged with having conducted medical experiments on inmates of concentration camps.

2. **The Milch Case:** Allegations of forced labor and medical experimentation at Dachau.

3. **The Justice Case:** Claims of abuses of legal processes within the Third Reich.

4. **The Pohl Case:** Charges directed against SS officers involved in the administration of concentration camps and in the use of forced labor.

5. **The Flick Case:** Prosecution of industrialists implicated in the confiscation of Jewish property and in the use of forced labor.

6. **The I. G. Farben Case:** Investigation of the leading chemicals manufacturer for offenses similar to those of the Flick case.

7. **The Hostages Case:** Charges relating to the ill treatment of civilians in southeastern Europe.

8. **The RuSHA Case:** Prosecution of officials of the SS Race and Settlement Office implicated in the policies of genocide.

9. **The Einsatzgruppen Case:** SS units charged with responsibility for mass murder.

10. **The Krupp Case:** Further charges of the exploitation of slave labor and confiscated properties.

11. **The Ministries Case:** Officials from the foreign office and other departments prosecuted for having been engaged in laying the diplomatic, economic, and other foundations for the Third Reich.

12. **The High Command Case:** Senior military figures charged with offenses against prisoners of war and against civilians in occupied areas.

In 1945 the world faced the problem of what to do about a Nazi regime that had presided over the extermination of some six million Jews and the deaths of millions of others with no basis in military necessity. Never before in history had the victors tried the vanquished for crimes committed during a war. Yet, never before in history had the vanquished perpetrated crimes of such monumental savagery. Thus, in 1945, in a rubbled world still smarting from the wounds of war, the specter of unprecedented Nazi horrors spurred a worldwide demand for unprecedented retribution. The Allies could hardly have turned a deaf ear to the outcry.

With the end of World War II, the time had arrived at last for humankind to translate the principles of morality into a legal cornerstone of international law that would outlaw and ultimately eliminate aggressive wars. The Allies had little choice but to seek out, prosecute, and punish Nazi war criminals. As suggested by author Ralph B. Perry:

> Had those responsible for the aggression and inhumanities of the Nazi regime been allowed to go unpunished, mankind would have lost a supreme opportunity to crystallize in legal form a recognized and pressing moral necessity. The time was ripe to step across the line from conscience to a legal order; and to create a legal precedent for future time.

The Allies, of course, stepped across that line—a line drawn in the blood of Nazi victims—and demanded that justice be done in the name of good peoples everywhere. Whitney Harris wrote:

> The proceeding at Nuremberg represented the seizure of a unique opportunity to convert vital moral principles into valid rules of law. And the supremacy of law was sustained and enforced by the Nuremberg process.

The Positive Side of Nuremberg

On the plus side of Nuremberg's legacy, the trials documented Nazi crimes for posterity. Many citizens of the world still remember growing up watching films of Nazi atrocities and reading grim accounts of Nazi brutalities. Two generations later, however, as many as 22 percent of Americans polled doubted that the Holocaust actually happened. But the facts—the reality of the Final Solution—are indelibly etched for all time in the forty-two-volume transcript of the Nuremberg trials.

Baldur von Schirach (with monocle) and son Klaus talk with newsmen after Schirach is released from Spandau Prison in Berlin after completing a twenty-year sentence.

Hundreds of official Nazi documents entered into evidence at Nuremberg tell the horrific tale of the Third Reich in the Nazis' own words. Six million Jews, and others adjudged undesirable by the Nazis, were indeed exterminated. Not one convicted Nazi denied that the mass killing had occurred. Each disclaimed only personal knowledge and responsibility.

"Another reward of Nuremberg," wrote historian Joseph E. Persico, "was to destroy any Nazi dreams of martyrdom. . . . The Third Reich was a foul creation, and the revelations at Nuremberg made that fact palpable." Arguably, this revelation led to the establishment of a democratic government in postwar Germany.

Nuremberg's Negatives

Charges of ex post facto law, the lack of legitimate jurisdiction, and victors' justice persist in marring the bright intentions of the Nuremberg proceedings. The establishment of the International Military Tribunal has yet to lead to a permanent counterpart before which crimes against peace and crimes against humanity can be tried. Despite twenty-four wars between nations and ninety-three civil wars or insurgencies between 1945 and 1992, no international body had been convened to try aggressor nations or individuals accused of war crimes.

In 1993, however, the UN Security Council finally acted to establish the first international criminal tribunal: the International Criminal Tribunal for Yugoslavia. It was expanded the following year to cover Rwanda, Africa. The Yugoslavia Tribunal promptly indicted twenty-one Bosnian Serbs. It has since taken measures leading to the indictment of Bosnian Serb leader Radovan Karadzic and General Ratko Mladic. But the means to prosecute and punish aggression rest still on the wavering will of an international community ever reluctant to impose sanctions on offending governments.

Spanning the Gap

Despite the reluctance of nations to unite in common cause and move swiftly toward a lasting deterrent to aggression, hope yet abides for the fulfillment of Nuremberg's brightest promise. In the fall of 1994, the UN recommended the establishment of a *permanent* International Criminal Court. So far, the proposal has progressed slowly and lacks enforcement provisions. Even so, the proposal lays one more beam in a bridge that may one day span the gap between rightful accountability and victors' justice.

The Nuremberg debates may continue for decades. But because of the tribunal's rulings at Nuremberg, the initiating and waging of aggressive war is now irrefutably criminal under international law. And that in itself is not a bad legacy.

Glossary

Big Three: Churchill, Roosevelt, and Stalin; also their respective nations, Great Britain, the United States, and the Soviet Union.

chancellor: Germany's head of state.

de facto: Actual.

European Axis Powers: Germany, Italy, Romania, Bulgaria, and Hungary.

ex post facto: Done, made, or formulated after the fact (as ex post facto law).

Final Solution: The Nazi program for the extermination of all Jews in Europe; *see also* Holocaust.

Four Power nations: The United States, Great Britain, France, and the Soviet Union.

gauleiter: Political district leader.

Gestapo: *Geheime Staatspolizei*, or Secret State Police.

Holocaust: The mass slaughter of European civilians, especially Jews, by the Nazis during World War II; *see also* Final Solution.

in absentia: In absence.

International Military Tribunal (IMT): The military tribunal for trying Nazi war crimes and criminals.

Kristallnacht: The night of November 10–11, 1938, during which roaming mobs of Germans, led by the Nazi Brownshirts, smashed the windows of Jewish shops (hence the name Night of Broken Glass) all over Germany. The Germans looted, burned, and generally devastated the Jewish shops in retaliation for the murder of a Nazi official, allegedly by a seventeen-year-old Jewish boy.

Lebensborn: A term meaning "fountain of life"; applied to Hitler's plan to accelerate the birth of "racially sound" babies.

Lebensraum: Living space; the term and policy for Nazi expansionism.

London Agreement: An agreement drafted by Four Power representatives at Church House in London, establishing the governing principles for prosecuting war crimes and criminals; issued on August 8, 1945, it formed the basis for the charter of the *International Military Tribunal* and the subsequent Nuremberg trials.

Low Countries: Belgium, Luxembourg, and the Netherlands.

Luftwaffe: German air force.

Nacht und Nebel: German for "Night and Fog"; phrase given to Hitler's order to seize persons "endangering German security" in the West and make them disappear into the night and fog of the unknown in Germany.

Nazi Party Leadership Corps: Leadership officials of the Nazi Party, down to the level where policy making ceased.

Nuremberg Laws: The two anti-Semitic laws issued by the Nazis in Nuremberg in 1935.

OKW: Initials derived from *Oberkommando der Wehrmacht,* the German Armed Forces High Command.

Reich cabinet: Ordinary cabinet ministers, members of the Council of Ministers for Defense of the Reich, and of the Secret Cabinet Council.

Reichsbank: Bank of Germany.

Reichschancellery: German headquarters.

Reichstag: German parliament.

SA: *Sturmabteilungen,* or Storm Troopers; early Nazi paramilitary organization established by Hitler in 1920 and dissolved in 1934; these storm troopers were also known as Brownshirts.

SD: *Sicherheitsdienst,* or security service (of the Nazi Party).

SS: *Schutzstaffel,* or protection squads; the SS, more than any other organization, symbolized Nazi arrogance and criminality.

Wehrmacht: German army.

Timeline

1939

September 1: Germany invades Poland; World War II begins.

1940

January: Word of Nazi atrocities filters out of Europe.

1942

January 13: Nine governments-in-exile meet in London and issue the St. James Declaration renouncing war crimes and promising to punish offenders.

1943

November 1: Churchill, Roosevelt, and Stalin issue the Moscow Declaration, affirming the St. James Declaration.

1945

April 12–June 26: Representatives of Free World nations meet in San Francisco to establish the United Nations.

May 7–8: World War II ends in Europe.

August 8: London Agreement signed by Four Power nations at Church House in London.

November 20: Allied prosecution of twenty-two Nazi war criminals begins in Nuremberg before the IMT.

1946

March 4: Allied prosecution ends.

March 8: The German case for the defense begins.

June 28: German defense ends.

September 30–October 1: Tribunal renders verdicts; trials end.

October 15: Göring commits suicide.

October 16: Ten condemned Nazis hanged.

November 1946–April 1949: Twelve additional trials of lesser Nazi war criminals held before U.S. military tribunals in Nuremberg.

For Further Reading

Joseph Bendersky, *A History of Nazi Germany*. Chicago: Nelson-Hall, 1985. An in-depth look at Germany in transition and the circumstances enabling Adolf Hitler's rise to power.

John Bradley, *The Illustrated History of the Third Reich*. New York: Grosset and Dunlap, 1978. An engrossing, profusely illustrated account of Germany's Third Reich, with particular emphasis on the war years.

Miriam Chaikin, *A Nightmare in History: The Holocaust 1933–1945*. New York: Clarion Books, 1987. A thorough accounting of the Nazi vendetta against Jews in Hitler's Germany.

Konnilyn G. Feig, *Hitler's Death Camps: The Sanity of Madness*. New York: Holmes and Meier, 1979. A grim, lucid account of life in the Nazi death camps featuring firsthand remembrances of camp survivors.

Robert Payne, *The Life and Death of Adolf Hitler*. New York: Praeger, 1973. An engaging, highly readable account of Germany's ruthless dictator, including rare letters and photographs.

Anthony Read and David Fisher, *Kristallnacht: The Unleashing of the Holocaust*. New York: Peter Bedrick Books, 1989. A stirring re-creation of the event that initiated Hitler's war against the Jews. The authors call on many eyewitnesses to authenticate their account of the "Night of Broken Glass."

Gail B. Stewart, *Hitler's Reich*. San Diego: Lucent Books, 1993. The author brings Hitler's Germany to life in a fresh account of the twelve-year regime that changed the world forever; contains many primary source quotations and interesting facts rarely seen in young adult publications.

Works Consulted

Winston S. Churchill, *Closing the Ring*. Boston: Houghton Mifflin Company, 1951. The fifth volume of Churchill's superlative six-volume history of the Second World War.

Robert E. Conot, *Justice at Nuremberg*. New York: Harper & Row Publishers, 1983. Reprint, New York: Carroll & Graf Publishers, 1994. The author reconstructs in an absorbing narrative style both the alleged crimes of the accused and the subsequent courtroom events at Nuremberg.

André Corvisier, ed., *A Dictionary of Military History*. Paris: Presses Universitaires de France, 1988. Reprint, Cambridge, MA: Blackwell Publishers, 1994. From the Battle of Actium to Zhukov, this scholarly volume offers a worldwide history of armed warfare, including an illuminating section on the laws of war.

Istvan Deak, "Misjudgment at Nuremberg," *New York Review of Books*, vol. 40, no. 16, October 7, 1993, pp. 46, 48–52. Deak provides an approving review of Telford Taylor's *Anatomy of the Nuremberg Trials* but disagrees with Taylor's favorable assessment of the proceedings.

I. C. B. Dear and M. R. D. Foot, eds., *The Oxford Companion to World War II*. Oxford and New York: Oxford University Press, 1995. This single-volume masterwork on the greatest war in history contains "more than 1,700 entries—ranging from brief identifications to in-depth articles on complex subjects" bringing "the far-flung elements and events of the war into focus."

Klaus P. Fischer, *Nazi Germany: A New History*. New York: The Continuum Publishing Company, 1995. This book, ten years in the writing, ranks right next to William L. Shirer's *The Rise and Fall of the Third Reich* for its comprehensive, richly narrated history of Germany during the Hitler years.

Max Frankel, "Word & Image: The War and the Law," *New York Times Magazine,* May 7, 1995, pp. 48–49. The author, a survivor of the Holocaust, criticizes the Nuremberg trials. He maintains that because the Nazis had not violated existing international laws, the Allies produced a false image of justice at Nuremberg.

G. M. Gilbert, *Nuremberg Diary.* New York: Farrar, Straus & Giroux, 1961. Reprint, New York: Da Capo Press, 1995. The prison psychologist at Nuremberg provides a daily account of the trial.

Martin Gilbert, "How Justice Was Done at Nuremberg," *New York Times Book Review*, November 22, 1992, pp. 15, 16, 18. The noted British historian reviews Telford Taylor's book *The Anatomy of the Nuremberg Trials*. Gilbert delivers a favorable review and comments about the impact of the Nuremberg trials on today's would-be aggressors.

Anton Gill, *An Honourable Defeat: A History of German Resistance to Hitler, 1933–1945.* New York: Henry Holt and Company, 1994. Drawing on recent research and on interviews with the few remaining resisters and their families, Gill tells the story of the Germans, small in numbers but great of heart, who secretly resisted the scourge of Nazism.

Whitney R. Harris, *Tyranny on Trial: The Evidence at Nuremberg.* Dallas: Southern Methodist University Press, 1954. Reprint, New York: Barnes & Noble (by arrangement with Lou Reda Productions), 1995. Professor Harris, one of the prosecutors at Nuremberg, draws on the great quantity of evidence gained from the proceedings there in 1945–46 to produce a single-volume testament to the Allies' attempt to, in Harris's words, "elevate justice and law over inhumanity and war."

Robert Jay Lifton, *The Nazi Doctors: Medical Killing and the Psychology of Genocide.* New York: Basic Books, 1986. Lifton's remarkable treatise stands unsurpassed as an examination into the darkest regions of the human psyche.

Frank McLynn, *Famous Trials: Cases That Made History.* Pleasantville, NY: The Reader's Digest Association, 1995. This fascinating volume offers vivid re-creations of thirty-four famous trials spanning two thousand years.

Joseph E. Persico, *Nuremberg: Infamy on Trial.* New York: Viking Penguin, 1994. Reprint, New York: Penguin Books, 1995. Persico describes the trial of the Nazi warlords of World War II in chilling character sketches and insightful observations about law and vengeance.

Tina Rosenberg, "From Nuremberg to Bosnia," *The Nation,* vol. 139, no. 3, May 15, 1995, pp. 688, 690, 692. Rosenberg examines the modern-day relevance of the prosecution of war criminals at Nuremberg from 1945 to 1949.

Gita Sereny, *Albert Speer: His Battle with Truth.* New York: Alfred A. Knopf, 1995. Of Sereny's rich and revealing work, Telford Taylor wrote: "A totally absorbing and tremendously important book, an essential contribution to the history of the Third Reich, and of the individuals who managed it."

William L. Shirer, *The Rise and Fall of the Third Reich.* New York: Simon & Schuster, 1960. Published more than a generation ago, Shirer's masterwork remains the definitive history of Germany under Adolf Hitler.

Telford Taylor, *The Anatomy of the Nuremberg Trials.* New York: Alfred A. Knopf, 1992. Reprint, Boston: Little, Brown and Company, 1992. In this book, called "a masterly work of military and judicial history" by the *New York Times,* the chief prosecutor at Nuremberg recounts the trials as he "heard, saw, and otherwise sensed them at the time, and not as a detached historian working from documents."

Index

Picture Credits

About the Author

Earle Rice Jr. attended San Jose City College and Foothill College on the San Francisco peninsula, after serving nine years with the U.S. Marine Corps.

He has authored eighteen books for young adults, including fast-action fiction and adaptations of *Dracula*, *All Quiet on the Western Front*, and *The Grapes of Wrath*. Mr. Rice has written several books for Lucent, including *The Cuban Revolution* and seven books in the popular *Great Battles* series. He has also written articles and short stories and has previously worked for several years as a technical writer.

Mr. Rice is a former senior design engineer in the aerospace industry who now devotes full time to his writing. He lives in Julian, California, with his wife, daughter, two granddaughters, five cats, and a dog.